ISRAEL, THE CHURCH AND ISLAM

Israel, The Church and Islam

PAST, PRESENT AND FUTURE

Foreword by Dr Alec R. Passmore

Donald C.B. Cameron BTh, MA, PhD

40 Beansburn, Kilmarnock, Scotland

ISBN-13: 978 1 910513 30 9

Copyright © 2015 by John Ritchie Ltd.
40 Beansburn, Kilmarnock, Scotland

www.ritchiechristianmedia.co.uk

Scripture quotations marked "NKJV" are taken from the New King James Version®. Copyright© by Thomas Nelson, Inc. Used by permission. All rights reserved.

All rights reserved. No part of this publication may be reproduced, stored in a retrievable system, or transmitted in any form or by any other means – electronic, mechanical, photocopy, recording or otherwise – without prior permission of the copyright owner.

Typeset by John Ritchie Ltd., Kilmarnock
Printed by Bell & Bain Ltd., Glasgow

Contents

Foreword by Dr Alec R. Passmore	11
Abbreviations	14
Chapter 1 PHENOMENA OF COMPARATIVE RELIGION	15
1. A Doomsday Scenario	15
2. Islam in Perspective	27
3. Personal Experience of Muslim Society	22
4. Points to Bear in Mind in Discussion	24
5. Some Basic Contrasts	26
6. Islam – Waxing or Waning?	28
7. Islamophobia	30
8. Application of Bible Prophecy to Islam	31
9. Meanwhile in Many Churches	34
10. Certainties and Uncertainties	36
11. A Prophetic Overview	37
Chapter 2 A BRIEF HISTORY OF ISLAM	41
1. Islam and its Roots	41
2. The Geographical Setting	43
3. Muhammad The Man	43
4. Muhammad the Prophet and the Koran	46
5. Muhammad's Life Continued	48
6. The Spread of Islam	51
7. Christian Counter Attacks	52
8. Modern Islamic Reassertion and Expansion	55
Chapter 3 THE THEOLOGY OF ISLAM	61
1. The Koran and Hadiths	61
2. The Bible Pre-Dates the Koran	64
3. God and Allah Not the Same	65
4. The Moon God	68
5. The Holy Trinity	69

6. Islamic Understanding of the Birth of Jesus Christ .. 72
  7. The Divine Sonship of Jesus Christ 75
  8. The Koran and the 'Infancy Gospels' 77
  9. Islamic Denial of Christ's Death 80
  10. Salvation and the Pillars of Islam 83
  11. Beatitudes Which Islam Cannot Equal 87

Chapter 4   THE ANTECEDENTS OF TWO FAITHS 89
  1. Why Bother? 89
  2. From Adam to Abraham 90
  3. The Patriarch Connection 93
  4. Rivalry Between Ishmael's and Isaac's Mothers 94
  5. Contrasting Views of Abraham's Greatest Test 97
  6. What Actually Happened on the Mountain 100
  7. Isaac, Esau and Jacob 101
  8. Perceptions of Israel 102
  9. Galatians and Islam 105
  10. Descendants of Lot, Ishmael and Jacob 108

**Chapter 5   JERUSALEM'S TENANTS IN THE
                ICHABOD AGE** 111
  1. Jerusalem's Significance to Three Faiths 111
  2. Ichabod – Departed Glory 114
  3. The Departure of the Glory 116
  4. Dispersal and Crownlessness 118
  5. Subsequent Defilement of the Jerusalem Temple .. 119
  6. Islam – The Dominant Ichabod Age Presence 121
  7. Palestine, Transjordan and Israel 123
  8. The Interim Spiritual Situation 125
  9. Birth of a State Before Birth of a Nation 129
  10. Recent Years 131

Chapter 6   CONTRASTING EXPECTATIONS 134
  1. The Collective and Individual Future 134
  2. Afterlife 135
  3. Afterlife in the Old Testament 136
  4. The Future of Israel 137
  5. Afterlife in the New Testament 140
  6. The Future of the Church 142
  7. Afterlife in the Koran and Islamic Tradition 144

- 8. The Future of Islam 149
- 9. No Islamic Millennium 151

Chapter 7 THE DEMISE OF ANCIENT RELIGIONS AND FEUDING NATIONS 154
- 1. Israel and Islam in the Tribulation Period 154
- 2. Islamic End Time Prophecy 155
- 3. The Trinity of Evil 157
- 4. Mystery Babylon 159
- 5. Ten Kings Who Destroy Babylonian Religion 163
- 6. The Tribulation Temple 165
- 7. A Suicidal Northern Jihad? 169
- 8. Wars of the Great Tribulation 173
- 9. Israel's Nearer Neighbours 177
- 10. Armageddon – The Jerusalem Battle Front 179
- 11. An Islamic Antichrist? 181

Chapter 8 THE FUTURE AND PERSONAL OPTIONS .. 186
- 1. Taking Stock 186
- 2. Why the Delay in Judging? 188
- 3. God's Timing is Perfect 190
- 4. Your Personal Future? 192
- 5. Witnessing to Muslims 194
- 6. Witnessing to All Three 195

Bibliography 200

Foreword by Dr Alec R. Passmore

It is a special delight to commend the following pages of Donald Cameron's latest and unique contribution to the understanding of believers working to grasp a consistent Biblical world-view. I have found here essential information I have not found available elsewhere. Here, the words of an able student of Scripture bring the unerring light of God's Word to bear upon our troubled world. The Lord, speaking through the prophet Hosea in his days, lamented: "The LORD hath a controversy with the inhabitants of the land, because there is no truth, nor mercy, nor knowledge of God in his land". He also laments: "My people are destroyed for lack of knowledge..." (Hosea 4:6). Through the failure of many of their teachers and leaders, the people of Hosea's day were being robbed of the knowledge of God's word and will for the essential maintenance of their testimony. The strategy of our enemy is the same today!

How grateful we are for the following pages from the able pen of one who has held so closely to the inspired scriptures of truth! I am thankful for his clear teaching concerning the pre-tribulational and pre-millennial return of Christ. And how refreshing also to follow his teaching concerning the future of God's earthly people Israel!

In this very wide ranging survey of world trends, the treatment of the origins of the practice of Islam is most helpful. The writer speaks from personal experience and understanding of Muslim beliefs and teaching, having served as a young soldier in several Muslim lands, and been on active service in the war in Oman (1950's) in what were hints of the coming "Arab Spring". He has studied the theology of Islam well. Here we find a full and deeply studied discussion of the origins of Islam, the Koran and the Prophet. He does not shrink from bringing before his readers the uncomfortable threat faced today by Israel and the West. Here is essential knowledge for all who would understand and reach Muslims with the glorious Gospel of the Saviour's mercy and love. His "Points to bear in mind" in our witnessing to them includes the warning that "Islam is more than a religion, it is a religious-political-social system". The author's deep interest in the salvation of souls is plain in his conclusions.

Writing of the "Contrasting expectations" between the Christian Gospel and the claims of Islam, he ensures that the reader will be left in no doubt that they are far from being "sister religions". Bible salvation through the blood of the Lamb of God, the Jewish Messiah, is the only certainty for an eternal destiny with Jesus Christ. Contrasting expectations about the future of the Church of saved believers and the followers of Islam are similarly dealt with, as is the future of Jerusalem, the tinder box of the Middle East, and the entire world. Donald Cameron walks in the light of the Lord's revealed prophetic future and of the message of the near-return of Christ. This is unfashionable in much of today's Church, which like the secular world, asks "Where is the promise of His coming?" Of great help is the author's satisfying and helpful overview of Israel's Biblical and post-Biblical history, and the divine right of her Jewish tenants right up to this day, by the everlasting provisions of the Abrahamic covenant.

This book represents a unique work of reference for every leader and teacher of the Lord's flock. We shall return to it again and again. I commend this far-reaching resource to all who serve in the ministry of God's work, and for the undoubted personal edification of every believer.

Alec R. Passmore

Dr Passmore is Chairman of the Society for the Distribution of the Hebrew Scriptures (SDHS) and President of Prophetic Witness Movement International (PWMI – founded by Dr FB Meyer. He has preached on Bible prophecy throughout Great Britain and Ireland and widely in Europe.

ABBREVIATIONS

ASV	American Standard Version
AV (KJV)	Authorised Version, now often referred to as the King James Version
Dby	New Translation by JN Darby
NIV	New International Version
NKJV	New King James Version
NT	New Testament
OT	Old Testament
RSV	Revised Standard Version
RV	Revised Version
YLT	Young's Literal Translation

CHAPTER ONE

Phenomena of Comparative Religion

So shall I have wherewith to answer him that reproacheth me: for I trust in thy word.
(Ps 119:42).

1.1. A DOOMSDAY SCENARIO

A secular think tank, the Doomsday Clock, which includes seventeen Nobel laureates, announced in January 2015 that the minute hand had moved forward two minutes towards global catastrophe. In contrast to that, in thousands of churches they stubbornly persist in singing triumphalist 20th Century songs describing as imminent an idyllic scenario which the Bible plainly teaches is due to materialise only after the return of the Lord Jesus Christ.

International Islamophobia burgeons alarmingly, and is most loudly protested against by the very people who give rise to it, although many Muslims are perceptive enough to realise that it is mainly other Muslims who are responsible for making their faith increasingly odious to the rest of the world. In the meantime the problems are not going to go away, and it is surely the responsibility of all Christians, particularly at leadership level or close to the Christian-Islamic interface, to be aware of the Bible's position on these issues. Muslims may protest about the use of sniffer dogs to check for explosives on aircraft bound for the Middle East, on the grounds that these will render the planes ritually unclean for prayer during flights; but they are slow to admit that it is mainly the activities of other Muslims which make the sniffing necessary in the first place! Inconsistencies abound. It is fair to concede that in the media all Muslims tend to be tarred with the same brush. Non-militant Muslims in the West would be better, for their own sakes, to give up this self-activated persecution complex, which only fuels further insularity. We return to the topic of Islamophobia at 1.7.

A young British citizen of Kuwaiti extraction, Mohammed Emwazi or 'Jihadi John', transmits to the world his gloating beheading of several people, whose main 'crime' was simply to be Western or Christian. His friends in England react with shock, saying "what a beautiful young man he was, extremely kind, extremely gentle and most humble". They blame his radicalisation on the MI5 security service, who had had very good grounds indeed to investigate him, but who, in a country which is much more likely to give Muslims the benefit of the doubt than Christians would receive in the average Muslim country, allowed him to go free. But all this will inevitably reinforce Islamophobia; the cycle of action and reaction is hardly set to come to an end within the foreseeable future; rather it is yet another facet of the accelerating signs of the times.

In February 2015 Archbishop Bashar Warda of Iraq warned that, without foreign military aid, there would very soon be no Christians left in Iraq. Isis was already practising genocide on those who refused to convert to Islam. Students of Bible prophecy cannot be quite as precise as the so-called Doomsday clock claims to be, but they would have to be blind not to realise from dozens of Scriptural passages that the return of the Lord Jesus Christ must be drawing very close indeed. It is wrong, and indeed cowardly, for Christians to adopt a blinkered approach when millions are suffering. We are today witnessing phenomena which may be modified or intensified, but will not go away this side of our Lord's return.

It would be easy to erect an Islamic Aunt Sally and throw stones at it. It would be easy nowadays to blame Islam for all the world's evils; but it would not be honest. I believe that it will be much more effective to declare the prior Biblical position on a number of major issues, and to see how Islam measures up to these. We should be analytical, but not emotional; emotion can cloud judgment.

Approaching Islam with an attitude of unassailable moral superiority is most unwise. In writing this book I have frequently encountered factors, some of which I had not previously noticed, where Jews and Christians have encouraged Muslims to believe that it is they who occupy the moral high ground, rather than we. We will see examples as we proceed. I wish periodically in this book to demonstrate that in many ways Christians are unconsciously aiding and abetting Muslims in the advance of Islam. If we are aware, we can do something about it.

We will see much about Islamic society and Islamic nations; but we dare not generalise about individuals, each one of whom, like the rest of us, is personally accountable to God. Each should be thought of as a soul who can be won for Christ.

1.2. ISLAM IN PERSPECTIVE

Comparisons in this book will be drawn mainly between Israel and Islam and between the Church and Islam; though sometimes Israel and the Church together will be compared with Islam. To include comparisons between Israel and the Church would widen our scope too much. In the Old Testament, in anticipation of the Cross, God provided the perfect way for sinful mankind to be reconciled to Himself. In the New Testament, on the basis of the now completed work of the Cross, He still offers a perfect way. But in either case the reconciling righteousness is imputed. Therefore we must approach Muslims from a position of humility, our righteousness not being our own. Only by identifying with Paul's declaration, have we any right to boast: *"But God forbid that I should glory, save in the cross of our Lord Jesus Christ, by whom the world is crucified unto me, and I unto the world"* (Gal 6:14).

A few decades ago in British schools the subject of Religious Knowledge, depending upon the curriculum, was almost entirely based upon Christian teaching and the Bible. Now our children are more likely to be taught 'Comparative Religion', and in most schools the teaching that one religion is more valid than another is forbidden. Comparing Christianity with Islam, whether within an educational curriculum or not, is fraught with difficulties, because it can never be a case of comparing like with like, although casual observers may assume that it is. At an 'organisational' or 'structural' level both Christianity and Islam are deeply fragmented. Most readers will have enough knowledge of church history to understand the main divisions within Christianity. In subsequent chapters we will see something of the main divisions within Islam; however in this first chapter it will be convenient to think of Islam as a united front.

The art of contending for our faith without compromising, and of presenting Christ in a way that is both challenging and appealing, can be acquired and developed only with wisdom, patience and prayer. This book is intended to be helpful to those who want to witness to, or who have to live among, Muslims, as well as to Muslims who wish to know how the Bible relates to the three faiths covered.

Although in certain lands where Christianity and Islam rub shoulders, Christians are being murdered, tortured and subjected to intense pressures to convert to Islam, many Muslims are in fact becoming Christians – are being saved! We cannot even guess at the numbers. Long ago Elijah complained to God: *"I, even I only, am left; and they seek my life, to take it away"* (I Kings 19:14); Evil Queen Jezebel was just as murderous as the most hardened Jihadist. But God was able to reassure the old prophet: *"Yet I have left me seven thousand in Israel, all the knees which have not bowed unto Baal"* (v 18). God knows every Christian believer in those lands where converting to Islam is a capital offence. Radio and satellite television allow at least some to listen to and even see the Gospel being preached in the comparative secrecy of their homes. And God looks not only into homes, but into hearts.

Recently there has been more internal resentment, particularly among women denied what are elsewhere regarded as basic human rights, such as education; and in those Muslim lands with active social media there have been demonstrations and rallies when restrictions have made normal life unbearable. Through His persecuted Church, God is witnessing in a way which even Satan cannot counter. Jesus' words that *"The time cometh, that whosoever killeth you will think that he doeth God service"* (Jn 16:2), is not limited to Muslims; in times past that has sometimes applied to Jews and fellow 'Christians' as well. However we must remember that today atrocities are being committed against fellow Muslims as much as against those of other faiths. Sometimes this persecution of Christians is counter-productive for the perpetrators. For instance in Lebanon Syrian Muslim refugees, nauseated by the cruelty they have witnessed on both Islamic sides in the land from which they have fled, have been attending Christian churches.

I possess books which are written for those who want to win Muslims for Christ; I have others which are written to expose Islam as a false faith, given to the persecution of others and a source of international conflict. This book contains elements of both. But I am equally conscious of the fact that seeking to evangelise Muslims can be a difficult and even dangerous pursuit, and that for many centuries what calls itself Christianity has been far from guiltless in its relationship with Islamic states and society. The gratuitous obscene cartoons of the gutter press's satirical magazines are directed against those held in reverence by Christians as well as against Muhammad. But Muslims are understandably incensed, and their faith is leading at least a few of them to commit atrocities in response, with disregard to the consequences for innocent bystanders, which Christians would regard as totally unacceptable. This kind of abuse of the freedom of the press and liberty of expression has no Christian basis; any society without self-discipline is doomed. It is utterly inappropriate to make fun of a religion which over a thousand million people take seriously.

In Chapter 2 we will look at how Islam and the Koran came into being, and in Chapter 3 we will consider the teachings of the Koran in greater depth. Many Islamic words are Arabic or derived from the Arabic. Transliteration into our Roman alphabet is therefore difficult, and renderings will vary, even among Islamic writers. We have long talked of the 'Koran', the holy book of Islam; but nowadays are likely to encounter such spellings as 'Qur'an' etc, However I will stick to the 'Koran' spelling, as Muslims tend to use that when addressing Christians. Also I am using the spelling 'Muhammad', but here again there are variations. I will use familiar spellings such as 'Mecca,' as opposed to 'Makkah', 'Medina' as opposed to Madinah and Hejira as opposed to Hijrah. Note that many Islamic books avoid frequently mentioning the name 'Muhammad', and prefer to say 'the Prophet'. I am using the Saheeh International version of the Koran by Al-Muntada Al-Islami, which is very helpful in that it uses spellings familiar to us for Bible names, such as Jesus and Mary, rather than A'isa and Mariam or Maryam. The frequent explanations in square brackets have been by inserted by Muslims to the text to clarify the Islamic interpretation or understanding.

When I refer to 'Christianity' and 'Christians' without further qualification or quotes, I usually mean fundamental Bible-believing Christianity and converts. But sometimes in this book – and the context will indicate one way or the other – I shall use it in a wider sense to cover even nominal Christianity and nominal Christians. True Christians are those who believe in the salvation from sins through the sacrificial and vicarious death of the Lord Jesus Christ, the incarnate Son of God, as presented in two classical Bible passages, taken at face value, namely:
- *"For God so loved the world, that he gave his only begotten Son, that whosoever believeth in him should not perish, but have everlasting life"* (Jn 3:16)

- *"Let this mind be in you, which was also in Christ Jesus: Who, being in the form of God, thought it not robbery to be equal with God: But made himself of no reputation, and took upon him the form of a servant, and was made in the likeness of men: And being found in fashion as a man, he humbled himself, and became obedient unto death, even the death of the cross. Wherefore God also hath highly exalted him, and given him a name which is above every name: That at the name of Jesus every knee should bow, of things in heaven, and things in earth, and things under the earth; And that every tongue should confess that Jesus Christ is Lord, to the glory of God the Father"* (Phil 2:5-11).

Not only do these two passages reflect some of the fundamental beliefs of true evangelical Christians, but, they are also invaluable in emphasising the differences between what Muslims and we believe about Jesus Christ – His pre-incarnate glory, His incarnation, suffering, exaltation and vindication, and, most of all, the love of God to which Muslims are strangers. We return to the Philippians quote in Chapter 3.5.

Except where otherwise indicated, I shall, as in the above verses, be using the Authorised or King James Version, which allows copious quoting without copyright problems. Muslims, because the Arabic of the Koran is also 'dated', should have no problems here. I will explain my fairly common use of certain other versions in Chapter 3.

As already stated, this book is intended, among other things, to give guidance as to how Muslims may be influenced for Christ. Inevitably this must involve exposing error; the Bible never compromises with error, and neither should we. But at least this can be done in a thoughtful way which will make people stop, listen and think, allowing God's Holy Spirit to speak through the Scriptures. It is God's place, not ours to exercise vengeance. Assertiveness is a strength and encourages listening. Both aggressive and apologetic behaviours, when dealing with spiritual truths and errors, are weaknesses and encourage opposition. Maintaining a balance is essential. Winning an argument at an intellectual level can mean losing a listener; and that, when we are dealing with eternal matters, can mean losing a soul.

We may find ourselves in circumstances where contending for the faith is both natural and necessary. Door-to-door visits by representatives of Islam will never happen, as with some of the cults. On the other hand, choosing to go out to seek opportunities to witness to Muslims is not an easy option. The most effective witness for Christ in Muslim countries may, in extreme cases, be the choice by local believers of martyrdom, often by beheading or sometimes even by crucifixion, or lesser, but nevertheless costly social and financial penalties, for refusing to convert to Islam. *"Precious in the sight of the LORD is the death of his saints"* (Ps 116:15). Those *"beheaded for the witness of Jesus, and for the word of God"* are singled out as participants in the blessed first resurrection. (Rev 20:4,6). God honours the witness of His own, and only eternity will reveal the size of the harvest of souls being reaped.

Within our own traditionally and nominally Christian land, our best witness is to live scrupulously honest, sincere and consistent lives, and to be unashamed to honour and talk about our God and Saviour (we will discuss such titles in Chapter 3).

1.3. PERSONAL EXPERIENCE OF MUSLIM SOCIETY

I am not without first-hand experience of Islamic society in its homelands. Missionary work among Muslims has always been difficult and sometimes lonely activity. Many years ago, as a young soldier, I had the privilege of visiting and sharing fellowship with missionaries in the Trucial Oman before the discovery of oil, when it was still a poor land, without as much as mains electricity in the main towns. Later it became the super-rich United Arab Emirates. In Bahrain a fellow soldier and I once stood with a missionary, keeping a low profile in the shadow of a doorway

Phenomena of Comparative Religion

and witnessed a Ramadan torchlight procession, where some of the young male participants were practising self-flagellation for the crimes of their ancestors. I had never before experienced such a palpable atmosphere of evil. Also I was on active service in the brief 1957 Jebel Akhdar war in Oman, when the Sultan asked Britain to support him against the Imam, who was keen to annex the Sultanate, or at least part of it, to predatory Saudi Arabia; it was one of the early hints of the later 'Arab Spring'. The small detachments of British troops were in these countries by invitation of their rulers for peace keeping purposes. A year later only the fact that I was due to be posted back to Scotland saved me from being sent with my battalion in July 1958 to Jordan to support against Ba'athist Islamic extremists, who had just overthrown two similar regimes in Syria and Iraq, a Hashemite king who had been born in Mecca and claimed, probably with some justification, to be directly descended from Muhammad and Fatima.

During the course of my Army service I met many Muslims sent to Britain on secondment or on military courses. It was then widely recognised in the Services that little if any attention was paid by many of these to Shariah Law and Muslim customs, free from the watchful eyes of mullahs, imams or other authorities. Forty years ago I witnessed young Muslim officers arrive in Britain, flush with money, buying hundred pound bags of coins to feed 'one armed bandits' or gambling machines, because gambling is forbidden in Islam. I have seen similar inconsistent behaviour in civilian life as well – Muslims who were quite happy to ignore the dietary restrictions of Ramadan at coffee breaks, for instance, provided they were certain that there was nobody to report them. Islam probably has quite as many hypocrites as the more apostate elements of Christianity; but we are not in a position to judge. I am merely commenting upon supposed moral high ground. It is probably safer to be a religious hypocrite in a Christian country than in a Muslim one where Shariah Law reigns supreme. After I retired from the Army I sometimes helped a mission in Berkshire which was seeking to evangelise Asian communities, although the work was more successful with Hindus than with Muslims.

1.4. POINTS TO BEAR IN MIND IN DISCUSSION

When talking with Muslims, it is important to keep certain facts in mind, without necessarily voicing them, in order to help level a very uneven playing field, which is full of misunderstandings and misconceptions. Many of the following are not good starting points if we wish to engage in profitable discussion; however true they may be, some will immediately 'pull down the blinds' if we apply them. They can be introduced later, or simply used unobtrusively to channel our discussion. Several of these points we will expand later:-

- Islam is more than a religion. It is a religious-political-social system, and its adherents tend to think of other faiths in the same ways. Strictly speaking there is no such thing as a Christian country, as that title would imply that all citizens are true believers. But I use the term loosely to distinguish them from countries which have other predominant religions. Muslims tend to assume that anybody in a traditionally Christian country who does not claim any other religion or claim atheism is automatically a Christian. In fact nowadays probably only around ten percent (precise statistics do not matter here) of those who fit that description can be even loosely classed as committed Christians, while even fewer seem to be true believers. The fact that our Bible contains the Old Testament, where Israel as a nation had a unique covenant relationship with God, with immediate consequences of blessing and cursing for obedience and disobedience, does not mean that this also applies to Christians, who live in an alien world with no such covenant. We return to this in Chapter 4.8.
- In contrast with the above, evangelical Christians believe that nobody is a true Christian without having first placed true saving faith in the redemptive work of the Lord Jesus Christ; whereas most Muslims believe

that anybody born into a Muslim family is automatically a Muslim, even though not necessarily a good Muslim. Admittedly Islamic doctrine does not fully support this, but is the common perception.

- Most Muslims have very little awareness of even the most major differences between different Christian denominations and the vaguely Christian cults.
- Understandably Muslims tend to think of Christianity and the Lord Jesus Christ in terms dictated by the Koran. Now, whatever Muhammad may have said about actual Christians, the Koran does give some recognition to Christianity itself as Muhammad understood it, and to the fact that Jesus was miraculously conceived. Jesus is recognised by Islam as a prominent prophet, but emphatically not as the Son of God. We look at this in Chapter 3.
- In the same way that Christianity has, down through the centuries, become split among many factions in doctrines and traditions, so Islam was split following the death of Muhammad between what are often referred to as Shi-ite and Sunni Muslims. Other small groups exist. Particularly when we come to prophecy, it is useful to establish the branch of our contact. Muslim commentators and theologians have long had different interpretations, even of some portions of the Koran.
- A critically important point, which we shall enlarge upon in Chapter 3, is the fact that we do **not** mean the same Person when we talk about 'God'. Muslims assume that we worship the same deity as they do, but in a different way, and that the only real difference is that they call him 'Allah'.
- Muhammad recognised Adam, Noah, Abraham, Ishmael, Moses, John the Baptist and Jesus as prophets. What these are recorded in the Bible as having said Muhammad either acknowledged or denied as suited his personal interpretations.
- For any nation, warfare in defence of the realm is

legitimate. But otherwise, warfare for Christians means being unfaithful to one's religion and contrary to one's conscience, whereas for Muslims physical conflict, especially against 'infidels', is actually being obedient to one's religion, and may even ease the conscience of those who would naturally prefer a quiet life and prosperity.

1.5. SOME BASIC CONTRASTS

Some Christians may see Islam as being less alien to Christianity than certain Oriental religions such as Hinduism, Buddhism, Taoism and Shintoism, because it is Monotheistic, rejects idols, recognises Abraham as a God-ordained patriarch and even accepts that Jesus' birth was miraculous. However, as we shall see later, these apparent similarities are very limited when explored more fully. Paradoxically Muslims encounter within what they see as Christianity both idolatry and polytheism. So we must tread very carefully, and be aware of our vulnerability within a Post-Christian society.

When we compare the Christian derived cults with Christianity, departures tend to start from the New Testament. When Muslims compare Islam with Christianity, it is often from the oral traditions of what they assume the Bible to say, rather than from the actual text.

Paul wrote to Timothy: *"From a child thou hast known the holy scriptures, which are able to make thee wise unto salvation through faith which is in Christ Jesus. All scripture is given by inspiration of God, and is profitable for **doctrine, for reproof, for correction**, for instruction in righteousness"* (II Tim 3:15-16). Other tools may occasionally be useful in contending for the faith, but Holy Scripture is not only invaluable, but essential, because it is Holy Spirit breathed, and we dare not contend without it. The Prophet Muhammad held our Scriptures in some reverence and referred to both Jews and Christians as 'People of the Book', recognising that they had at least received some spiritual insight,

Phenomena of Comparative Religion

whatever else negative he and his followers might have said. Therefore we can quote our Bibles in discussion with Muslims, who are likely to disagree only when the Bible and the Koran conflict, which admittedly is rather often!

At first sight there might appear to be some common ground with evangelical Christianity in the following statement from a Muslim source intended to be read by non-Muslims:

> "Being a Muslim is essentially a very personal experience. It cannot be done 'second hand'. It involves a moment known as *ihsan* or realisation of being 'born anew'. Every Muslim has to experience that if their Islam is to be a truly living thing."

Now Orthodox Jews in Jesus' time on earth talked about a variety of second births, as at coming of age, (Bar Mitzvah), reaching the priestly age of thirty, etc. But Jesus told Nicodemus of a being born again which even that *"teacher of Israel"* could not comprehend (Jn 3:10). A central theme of New Testament Christianity is that one does not become a true believer or Christian *until* one has been born again. In contrast a Muslim remains a Muslim whether he has experienced *ihsan* or not, as is borne out by the capital offence in the eyes of Islam of somebody born into a Muslim family or Muslim society converting to another religion.

For a Christian, being born again is a transaction of eternal consequence, not merely a 'commitment' which can be broken, or some other form of religious experience. It involves recognition that our salvation is the gift of God and not earned. For the Muslim, *ihsan*, however admirable it may appear to be, "is the Muslim responsibility to obtain perfection or excellence in worship". Again, one can hardly blame the Muslim for failing to see in what claims to be Christianity the stupendous contrast. We will see more of the contrasts between salvation in Christianity and in Islam at 3:10.

1.6. ISLAM – WAXING OR WANING?

Holy war, using the strange Muslim interpretation of holiness which condones atrocities, began with Muhammad, as a means of bringing the world into subjection to Muhammad's god. After centuries of mixed fortunes, Muslims now see a resurgence of this holy war or *jihad*, and are happy when Muslims show tendencies towards dominance in non-Muslim nations. We react with horror to teenage girls eagerly leaving the safety of European society to join *jihadists,* and to subject (and 'subject' is the appropriate word) themselves to what they see as heroes of Islam. But for them there is a certain glamour in such a risky enterprise; we may criticise them for many things, but not for their devotion to what they see as duty.

Whatever we may believe or wish to argue to the contrary, millions of Muslims world-wide believe that Islam is currently on the ascendency and Christianity in decline. Muslims see what they consider Christian nations overthrowing at parliamentary level and in the courts most of our former major Bible-based moral sanctions. In contrast, they see that the most fundamental and rigorous Shariah Law, which is based upon the sternest applications of the Koran, while far from universally applied within Islamic society, is gaining ground with those who would like to see it applied globally.

Christianity and Islam are the two world religions with a strong compulsion to evangelise or to convert the whole world. In 1897 Historicist eschatologist Dr Grattan Guinness, in his major work, *"The Approaching End of the Age"*, voiced the popular, but inaccurate, perception that Islam, more often referred to at the time as 'Mohammedanism', was very much on the decline as a major faith, particularly in view of the widely recognised decline of the Ottoman Empire. This was a general view, rather than a Bible-based one. Nearly a hundred and twenty years later, who would dare say that Islam is very much on the decline?

One increasingly common form of Islamic 'evangelisation' is the kidnapping of Christian girls, especially in Sunni Egypt and in West Africa, registering them as Muslims and forcing them to marry. Thus Islam is being made to stink in the nostrils of the world, because it does not take much knowledge of religion to know that such a method of 'conversion' must be repellent to a righteous God.

The recognition in 1948, mainly by 'Christian' nations, of the state of Israel within what had long been considered Muslim land, and the subsequent anti-colonial stance of such figures as Nasser in Egypt, gave some boost to Islamic expansion. In May 1948 the newly declared nation of Israel was, without declaration of war, immediately attacked by the sizeable well-equipped armies of five neighbouring states. But these were repulsed in what for them was a most humiliating defeat, still referred to as *Al Naqba* – the Calamity. The obvious answer that Israel's God was more powerful than theirs apparently did not occur to them. But what really fired more recent Islamic aspiration to conquer the world for Allah was the catastrophic, lightning defeat of splendidly equipped forces of Islamic nations by Israel in the 1967 Six Day War, which professional soldiers elsewhere recognised at the time as sheer brilliance by Israeli generals, and those of us who at the time were both professional soldiers and Bible-believing Christians recognised as primarily the hand of God.

To Muslims this defeat was a bitter humiliation, They could only conclude that it was Allah's punishment for their secularisation and religious lethargy. There was a surge of genuine repentance for inactivity and a revival of militancy, which, since that time has been in a state of continual revisionism and regional variation. There is still a massive thirst for revenge.

Although Islam is currently waxing rather waning, it is increasingly demonstrating the seeds of its own destruction; Jesus said: *"every city or house divided against itself shall not stand"* (Matt 12:25). We return to this at 7.11.

1.7. ISLAMOPHOBIA

'Phobia' is defined in Chambers' Dictionary as 'a fear, aversion or hatred, especially an irrational one.'

So immediately we have the problem of mixed perceptions. One may therefore very properly interpret Islamophobia as a **fear** of Islam, which, in view of what is happening around the world, is reasonable and fully understandable. On the other hand it may be seen as **hatred** of Islam; and, reprehensible though such hatred may be, even within Islam many recognise that many Muslims are bringing it upon their community by their actions.

Thousands of Muslims are fleeing from Islamic countries to the comparative peace, safety and prosperity of what they consider to be Christian countries. Muslim refugees pay exorbitant sums, sometimes all that they possess, to fellow Muslim profiteers for places on unseaworthy craft to cross the Mediterranean, and on the way they throw overboard the few Christians among their fellow-passengers. What do they expect that to tell the world about Islam?

The efforts of governments and legislatures to counter Islamophobia and racism, which are not the same thing despite some overlap, may be well-meaning, but are ineffective. Reconciliation is a positive reaction and appeasement a negative reaction to Jihadism; but neither works, because both are seen as weaknesses by Muslims. Mere law enforcement will fail miserably, when one considers that the Son of God foretold that this age will end with violence comparable with the days of Noah, when the whole earth was filled with violence (Gen 6:11, Matt 24:37).

It is all too easily forgotten that much of the violence in today's world has nothing to do with Islam. Inter-tribal warfare with no Islamic influence in southern Africa is growing. There has been a huge increase in recent years in the number of refugees from some Latin American nations, where Roman Catholicism is dominant, entering or trying to enter the United States in order

Phenomena of Comparative Religion

to escape the corruption and violence in their homelands, where, five hundred years before, the Conquistadores had imposed a ritualistic form of Christianity without any spiritual regeneration. And throughout history there have been outbursts of extreme violence in many other lands. What is different with the current form of Wahabist Islam (the term will be explained at 2.7.) and Jihadism is that they seek world domination through violence. They vow to destroy the United States, and some Americans actually think that the Bible teaches that they will succeed, simply because America does not specifically feature in end-time prophecy! The reason that America and many other countries do not feature in Bible prophecy has little or nothing to do with latter day Islam. It is because they are not within the territory of the ancient empires which once occupied the Holy Land. We will deal with this in Chapter 7.

During the coming Tribulation there will, as we have noted, be violence of a level unprecedented since the Flood. But, as we will see in Chapter 7.10., the indications are that the final source will not be Islamic. Christians may understand Islamophobia in others, but know that our God is in overall control and will, in His own time, thwart all the elaborate and ambitious plans of this world's warmongers, whoever they are. Our confidence is in our Lord's return for us before the darkest chapter in earth's history.

1.8. APPLICATION OF BIBLE PROPHECY TO ISLAM

Too many books on Bible prophecy seek to sell themselves by being sensational. Teachers of prophecy are required to be faithful rather than clever. In Chapter 7.6. to 7.9. we will see that what are currently Islamic nations feature prominently in end-time prophecy; but we will also see that some key matters are presented in the Bible in a way that should keep us alert, rather than fully confident. I shall not be claiming, for instance that the Antichrist is to be a Muslim. Some positive identifications will be given only to those who live through the end-time Tribulation Period; they will need to know.

The fact that most Christian books or booklets on Islam ignore both what our religion and theirs believe about the End Times was one of the factors which prompted me to write this book. A frightening number of Christians who style themselves as Bible-believing have less idea of what the Bible teaches about the latter days than many Muslims, particularly Shi-ites, have about what the Koran and the Hadiths teach about them. Many churches would scarcely notice were Christ's Olivet Discourse to be removed from their Bibles! This is shameful and can be traced right back to the great Augustinian lie, which so many of the Reformers swallowed or at least refused to refute; namely, that all Scripture should be taken as literally as possible, apart from unfulfilled predictive prophecy, which should be taken figuratively or allegorically. I have written at length in other books about this scandal, which is a slight against the Holy Spirit who inspired equally both the fulfilled and unfulfilled prophecies (think about that!), and wants to share God's plans for the planet with us. Christians are thus rendered vulnerable. The other great disincentive to take end-time prophecy seriously is Preterism, which claims that most of the end-time prophecies were fulfilled, sometimes in an obscure and diminished way, early in the Church Age, thus undermining the reliability of Scripture in the minds of readers, who may well assume that, if prophecy is highly exaggerated, much else in the Bible could be too.

However, particularly in Chapters 6 and 7, I do propose to make full use of prophecy, particularly eschatology or latter-day prophecy, for the following reasons:-

- The Bible's predictive prophecy is an invaluable yet under-used tool for contending for our faith.
- Predictive prophecy first occurs in Genesis chapter 3 and is frequently found between that point and Revelation chapter 22. It is no isolated theme in our Bible, but fully integrated with other doctrines.
- The Lord Jesus Christ Himself, whilst on earth, made many both short-term and long-term prophecies, and

many of these were for practical purposes as well as for warning, comfort or information.
- Any Muslims who have seriously sought to understand Christianity are likely to have encountered frightening ignorance of prophecy among church-goers. It is important that they should realise that our evangelical faith is supported by, rather than discredited by prophecy, and that many evangelicals do have strongly held, solidly based beliefs in Bible prophecy.
- Many prophetic Bible passages point clearly to the fact that the future is safely in God's hands, and that, although He is allowing mankind to take the planet to the brink of disaster, nothing can happen which is not within His permissive will.
- The current perilous state of the world makes many people bury their heads in the sand, seeking such pleasures as are available by whatever means they can find, and hoping that disaster will not strike within their lifetime. But others, particularly those who recognise the extent of modern moral decline and ecological disaster, may well be open to a truly convincing presentation of God's plan of the ages, with the further insight which this gives into the assurance of eternal life for believers, as well as to the medium term future of our planet. Let us remember that, although theirs is very different from ours, some Muslims have their own sincerely held agenda for dealing with the current state of the world.
- Courtesy, particularly initially, is essential for profitable contact. Courtesy is much easier to maintain if we are well grounded in our own beliefs, and this should include the major Bible theme of prophecy.
- Perhaps most importantly of all, there are sincere, generally Bible-believing Christians (I know some), who are convinced that sooner or later Islam must be eclipsed. They implicitly trust God for that. But, because of their extremely limited either Amillennial or Post-Millennial perspective of the Bible's revealed programme

for the future of the planet, a perspective which ignores the many detailed Tribulation Period prophecies of our Lord and His prophets, they are at a loss to see how or when this eclipse will be accomplished.

In all eight of my previous books I have devoted much more space to eschatology than to fulfilled prophecy; this time I will devote only a little more!. Predictive prophecy need not be confined to special sections; it is going to crop up periodically as we proceed. From Chapter 5 I shall devote considerable space to fulfilled prophecy, particularly within the contrasting branches of Abraham's descendants, which often confirms eloquently the superiority and reliability of our Holy Bible, and its relevance to current world events. End-time prophecy will feature prominently in Chapters 6 and 7.

1.9. MEANWHILE IN MANY CHURCHES.....

We need to ensure that we do not come under the same condemnation as the Emmaus disciples at Jesus' First Coming: *"Then he (Jesus) said unto them, O fools, and slow of heart to believe all that the prophets have spoken"* (Lk 24:25). There had been a reluctance among the disciples to accept that His crucifixion had to precede His vindication within His Messianic mission programme. As His Second Coming approaches, there is an equal reluctance within many churches to accept that the Tribulation Period must precede His Return in power and glory. As we saw in the previous section, **there is a grave danger of our interest in the end-time prophecies of our Scriptures being eclipsed by the interest displayed by Muslims in the prophecies in their sacred writings.** Surely that should not be! Even some evangelical churches come under the condemnation of the Pharisees and Sadducees: *"When it is evening, ye say, It will be fair weather: for the sky is red. And in the morning, It will be foul weather to day: for the sky is red and lowring. O ye hypocrites, ye can discern the face of the sky; but* **can ye not discern the signs of the times?**" (Matt 16:1-3).

Phenomena of Comparative Religion

During the second half of the 20th Century there was a great resurgence of Post-Millennialism within churches world-wide, something which had been in decline since the First World War. This resurgence peaked during the 'seventies and 'eighties, with an agenda based around the following false assumptions:-

- The moral and environmental state of the world was improving as the Lord's return approaches.
- The Millennium or righteous Kingdom, in which God's will will at last be *"done on earth as it is in Heaven"*, was now being or about to be achieved through the Church's carrying out with unprecedented vigour her Great Commission to evangelise the world.
- This enterprise was supposedly being enhanced by the restoration of the Church, a serious misunderstanding of Acts 3:2, which states clearly that Christ will remain in the Heavens **until** the *"Times of Restoration of all things"*. A comparison with Acts 1:6 confirms that **the restoration concerns Israel, not the Church**.
- The promised Millennium was now emerging either gradually or suddenly (views differed) from the current Church Age
- The world was therefore now beginning to be 'Christianised', meaning that most, though not all, would be saved
- Satan, having been 'bound since Calvary' and consequently already limited in his activity, would be much more restricted and less in evidence once this emerging new age was fully realised.
- This new age of world-wide spiritual enlightenment would end (not begin!) with the return in power and glory of the Lord Jesus Christ.
- Jesus Christ was not about to reign personally upon earth during the Millennium, but would do so through the Church in a way not previously seen.

The above is an extremely brief adaptation from chapter 9 of my book, *"The Millennium –Restoration After Retribution"*. Now look at the world around us!

That faithful prophet, Ezekiel, given by God tough messages to proclaim, complained bitterly of the same attitudes: *"Then said I, Ah Lord GOD! they say of me, Doth he not speak parables?"* (Ezek 20:49). Ezekiel would surely be equally frustrated by today's Preterists. Passages such as Lk 21:26-27 are conveniently ignored in Preterism and Post-Millennialism: *"Men's hearts failing them for fear, and for looking after those things which are coming on the earth: for the powers of heaven shall be shaken. And then shall they see the Son of man coming in a cloud with power and great glory"*. They would do well to remember who the Speaker was on that occasion.

Events of the first decade and a half of the 21st Century should serve as a timely reminder that we should be outdoing Muslims in our interest in our God's promises.

1.10. CERTAINTIES AND UNCERTAINTIES

On the rear cover of his book, *'The Signs of the Times'*, written in 1970, one finds the exemplary statement, "Dr Skevington Wood is careful not to exceed the limits imposed by the Word." In this chapter I also shall do my best not to 'exceed the limits imposed by the Word', in other words not to state as certainties facts which may be strongly hinted at or suggested in end-time prophecy, but are not as yet beyond reasonable doubt. The last chapter of Daniel is about events following the Rapture (not that Daniel as an OT saint was aware of the Rapture) but before the Lord's Return in Power. The final angelic message to Daniel was *"And he said, Go thy way, Daniel: for the words are closed up and sealed till the time of the end. Many shall be purified, and made white, and tried; but the wicked shall do wickedly: and none of the wicked shall understand; but the wise shall understand"* (Dan 12:9-10).

While there are many prophecies, some perfectly clear, about this future period, there are some things which will make sense only to those faithful souls who are living through them, and these will only be **spiritually discerned**. A specific example to

Phenomena of Comparative Religion

which we shall return at 7.3., is found in Rev 17:9 *"And here is **the mind which hath wisdom.** The seven heads are seven mountains, on which the woman sitteth."* Jesus imposed similar selective understanding when He said: *"It is given unto you **to know the mysteries** of the kingdom of heaven, but to them it is not given"* (Matt 13:11). *"For the LORD hath **poured out upon you the spirit of deep sleep, and hath closed your eyes:** the prophets and your rulers, the seers hath he covered"* (Isa 29:10). Judgmental blindness may be imposed by God, so that prophecy will make no sense to those who deliberately scorn it – **and that may apply even to believers.** No theological seminary can override the Lord's words, a factor which is frequently overlooked. The most brilliant logic in the world will not convince of truths, which the youngest child of God may grasp, where minds are determined not to believe. This sealing of Dan 12:9, as a number of commentators have pointed out, has been at least partially to ensure that these prophecies are preserved intact until they become absolutely vital to those living through their fulfilment, and evidently also so that they will escape the attention of those who scoff at them.

So I am not about to join the ranks of those who like to make sensational predictions, such as who the Antichrist will turn out to be; nor can I guarantee to say much **authoritative** about Islam as a religion after the Rapture, though we must devote a section (7.3.) to the demise, probably with all current false religions, of 'Mystery Babylon', which figures prominently during the Beginning of Sorrows. What we will see (7.7. to 7.9.), however, is that what are currently Islamic nations, some more clearly identifiable than others, certainly do feature during the seven plus years following the Rapture. And some are going to suffer huge military defeats.

1.11. A PROPHETIC OVERVIEW

Many readers will already be aware of the programme which I am summarising in this section. Others may be glad to have 'hooks to hang information on' – to see how the whole picture fits together, especially regarding how Israel and Islam are likely to feature in the End Times.

We may consider the unconditional future – what God has declared as being definite and not subject to negotiation - in four stages:
1. From now until the Rapture, when the Acceptable Year of the Lord (Isa 61:2, Lk 4:19) is to end. That could be at any moment.
2. The Tribulation Period, covering the Day of Vengeance of our God (Isa 61:2, Isa 63:4).
3. The Millennium or Year of the Lord's Redeemed (Isa 63:4).
4. The eternal state after this world has passed away (Rev 21:1).

At this stage I am giving no Scripture references, but will give many later when the need arises.
a. The world is not about to end, but the present Church Age could end at any time; individuals can be prepared for this by turning now in faith to the Lord Jesus Christ as their Saviour. The Church Age started on the Day of Pentecost, following a brief transitional period, which started when the veil in the Temple was rent at Christ's death.
b. This age will end with Jesus Christ raising the bodies of those of the Church Age who have died in faith, taking them to the place in Heaven prepared for them in a glorious incorruptible form. Believers still alive on earth will also be caught up and transformed in what is often called the Rapture – a term derived from a Latin translation of the New Testament.
c. Earth's darkest hour, which will follow this event, will last for little more than seven years. These seven years will be divided equally into the Beginning of Sorrows and the Great Tribulation. No more precise timescales are given in Scripture for this period, although some have tried to impose them.

Phenomena of Comparative Religion

d. There will be catastrophic wars, famines, climate changes, earthquakes, disasters, pandemics and terrifying cosmic happenings, all on an unprecedented scale. The Book of Revelation from Chapter 4 gives the heavenly viewpoint, and lists three series of signals or authorisations, namely Seals, Trumpets and Bowls or Vials of Wrath which start in sequence, but appear to end simultaneously with the Return in Power of the Lord Jesus Christ.

e. Two sinister emissaries of the Devil, namely the Beast and False Prophet (one of which is the final Antichrist, though there is a debate as to which) are to be extraordinarily active. They will exercise unprecedented power during their brief reign. After three and a half years the Beast will set up His Abomination of Desolation in Jerusalem and, aided and abetted by the False Prophet, will claim worship for himself and Satan.

f. Believers will be persecuted pitilessly and many will be martyred. Even in that dread age there will be many genuine opportunities for people to repent and find God, though with a real risk of incurring the wrath of the Beast and, consequently, martyrdom.

g. This Great Tribulation will end with the Battle of Armageddon, with 'ground zero' in the north of Israel, when Jesus Christ will visibly and physically return to earth in great glory, followed by saints and angels, to overthrow the Beast and his forces and to bind the Devil for a thousand years utterly beyond reach of mankind.

h. On earth Jesus Christ will conduct an assize, likened to a shepherd separating sheep and goats, to determine who among the survivors of earth's hugely depleted population will be allowed to enter in their mortal bodies the following peaceful thousand year reign.

i. Jesus Christ will rule for a thousand years (the Millennium) in absolute justice with a rod of iron. Those who have already died and been resurrected, plus those previously raptured, being immortal, will inhabit the New

Jerusalem which is to descend from Heaven, and which will be withdrawn at the end of the thousand years. The shattered environment which will emerge from the Great Tribulation will be restored and the earth will be repopulated. There will be no tempter, and, while sin will not be totally absent, lawlessness will not be permitted. All people will be required to worship Jesus Christ, but not all of those who will be born during the Millennium will have saving faith.

j. Following this Millennium, those born on earth during the thousand years will be tested for their acceptance or rejection of salvation. Those saved will inhabit a new earth. This earth and its immediate heavens will vanish for ever, to be replaced by imperishable new earth and heavens. The scrupulously fair final judgment of all unbelievers will take place; there will be two criteria, (1) Having names written in the Lamb's Book of Life – which no unbeliever will have, and (2) Works, which will render the Lake of Fire more tolerable for some than for others. So solemn is this evidently sensitive matter of degrees of eternal suffering, that only Jesus Christ Himself, whilst on earth, spoke of it.

The above summary has been adapted from my book, *"God's Timetable for a Troubled World"* (see Bibliography – also available on *Kindle*).

The next chapter is devoted to a brief history and background of Islam.

CHAPTER TWO

A Brief History of Islam

Jesus said unto them, Verily, verily, I say unto you,
Before Abraham was, I am.
(Jn 8:58)

2.1. ISLAM AND ITS ROOTS

This chapter requires care in preparation. Islam must not be misrepresented, either positively or negatively from the Christian point of view. However this is complicated by the fact that there is a good deal of revisionism within Islam regarding its own history. Their own early historians are sometimes ignored if their data is not complimentary. Before coming to key areas of doctrine, we must have some accurate, though not necessarily detailed, knowledge of Islam. I intend to keep this chapter brief, as plenty of fuller histories are available, both Islamic and non-Islamic; I am concentrating on those aspects which relate Islam to Israel and Christianity. In Chapter 5 there will be many more historical details, but only regarding Jerusalem.

By the end of the 6th Century AD much of the Christian world was in a spiritual state not unlike Israel and Judah before the Assyrian and Babylonian captivities of more than a thousand years earlier. In the west a succession of invading barbarian powers from the north, the worst of which were probably the Huns under Attila, had eventually adopted the religion of Rome, but successive invasions weakened the underlying Christian faith to the point where the Irish centred Celtic church had to send missionaries to France and Switzerland. Things in the East were little better, with only occasional reformers and some dreadful emperors like the brutal Phocas.

Dr Samuel Green in his Handbook of Church History, writes:
"But a cloud was now rising in the East, though as yet in size 'as a man's hand,' which was destined ere long..... to change the fortunes of the world. The virtues or the crimes of Eastern emperors, even the theology and spiritual claims of Roman bishops, sink into insignificance in comparison with the fact that an Arabian youth had some time before the close of the century married the rich widow of a former master, and was thus set free to ponder his mission, and to devise his plans. The name of the youth was Mohammed, that of his wife Kadijah."

This may sound a bit cynical, but it was very much the way in which Islam was perceived, and indeed, its military conquests were not unlike the aforesaid Assyrian and Babylonian invasions in Old Testament times. And those, the Bible makes it very clear, were permitted by God, although it was made equally clear that in God's good time the invaders themselves would be judged.

An awareness of the history of Islam makes it easy to see where their beliefs come from and will help to combat widespread ignorance. Ancient divisions within Islam are important. It is indeed the Religion of the Sword; but some Muslims are more militant than others, and we should beware of making sweeping statements, especially if we want to win some for Christ.

One may reasonably say that the history of Islam starts with Muhammad, but that the background dates back to the Patriarch Abraham and his family, something which we will look at in Chapter 4. Muhammad was born around 570 AD and died in 632. Muslims date their religion from the *Hijra* or *Hejira* or *Hegira* of 622 AD (see 2.5.), when their calendar starts, each year around October, being suffixed by the letters AH. Beyond doubt Muhammad was a remarkable man, whether one admires him or rejects him as a prophet of God. Most modern

A Brief History of Islam

Islamic histories of Muhammad attribute an amazing variety of virtues to him. Contemporary secular and even Islamic history, including his style of life and military tactics, might lead one to other opinions. This is in contrast to most of the Bible's heroes, where only Joseph (Genesis), Job and Daniel among the major characters have no fault recorded (see Ezek 14:14). Only the Lord Jesus Christ, the Son of God is stated in the Bible to be sinless; *"For he hath made him to be sin for us, who knew no sin; that we might be made the righteousness of God in him"* (II Cor 5:21). Neither Muhammad nor any other person in Islam has ever been sinless, thus to qualify as a vicarious sin-bearer.

2.2. THE GEOGRAPHICAL SETTING

It is helpful to know something of the cradle of Islam, which is a strip of dissected plateau from one to two hundred miles wide and over a thousand miles long, adjacent to the northern coast of the Red Sea. From ancient times until the 20th Century most settlements and towns were in oases, some large and very fertile, but separated by extensive arid land providing at best sparse grazing. Most of the inhabitants were tribal Arabs, though within the larger oasis towns there had been significant Jewish communities of traders and craftsmen for at least a thousand years before Islam, and smaller Christian communities for around half that time. Apart from some coastal shipping, communication and trading was, for safety in numbers and other practical reasons, mainly by caravan. Nomadic tribes, some of which made annual migrations north and back south, supplemented their income by extortion, ransom and protection money; caravans were considered fair game.

2.3. MUHAMMAD THE MAN

Muhammad was an Arab and the Koran is written in Arabic; translations into other languages are not held to have the same authority. It is widely accepted in the secular world that Arabs are the people who, with the exception of Israel, dominate the Arabian Peninsula as far north as central Iraq and Syria, North

Africa as far west as the Atlantic and as far east as the Horn of Africa. There are of course various minorities such as Berbers, Copts, Kurds and Ethiopians who pre-date Arabs within some of these lands. However most Muslims would define the term 'Arab' more strictly, and we could find Scriptural support. Arabs, like Jews are Semitic people, descendants of Shem, the son of Noah. Furthermore they claim a common ancestry from Abraham, through his son Ishmael; we will consider this in Chapter 4. Even in its early days, Islam spread far beyond the Arab world and now dominates nations as far east as Malaysia, Indonesia and even part of the Philippines. There have long been more non-Arab Muslims than Arab ones, and now Muslims may be found in every continent.

Muhammad's father died before he was born and his mother a few years later. He was brought up firstly by his grandfather, and then by his uncle. His family were members of the religiously influential Quraish (or Quarysh) tribe, who controlled the Ka'aba, the cube shaped shrine in Mecca, which, before Muhammad's time, contained numerous idols, icons and images. The society into which Muhammad was born contained both Jewish and Nestorian Christian groups, but was predominantly polytheistic, with no written laws and consequently a variety of beliefs, including variations of those practised by Israel's neighbours in Old Testament times. Muhammad can justly be given the credit for ending the polytheism.

If only those denominations which venerate images, icons, relics and religious trinkets appreciated the extent to which these non–Biblical features discredit Christianity, Islam might not be making such extensive inroads into Western society. Not surprisingly Jihadists see themselves as latter day Muhammads, cleansing a pagan world of idolatry.

The Ka'aba has, to this day, built into one of its walls, a much venerated black stone which was said to have fallen from heaven. It is evidently a meteorite, and perhaps was actually seen to fall from the sky. Muslims claim that it was built by Adam and, having been destroyed by a flood, was rebuilt by Abraham and Ishmael, an unlikely activity indeed for a tent dweller: *"By faith he (Abraham) dwelt in the land of promise as in a foreign country, dwelling in tents with Isaac and Jacob, the heirs with him of the same promise"* (Heb 11:9 NKJV). This had long been a place of pilgrimage, and many of the locals in Muhammad's time prospered by providing services for them.

The young Muhammad sometimes accompanied his uncle, who was a merchant, in trading caravans, reaching, it is thought, as far as Syria; but he also worked as a shepherd. His first wife, Khadijeh, many years his senior, died, leaving him only one surviving daughter, Fatima, of five children. Thereafter he had several wives, establishing the principal that one can have as many wives as one can afford – a policy somewhat tough on those who cannot afford even one in a society where there must inevitably be a shortage of eligible young ladies. Currently the limit of wives is generally four.

The Koran itself declares Muhammad to have been a sinner and in need of forgiveness: *"So be patient [O Muhammad]. Indeed, the promise of Allah is truth. And ask forgiveness for your sin and exalt [Allah] with praise of your Lord in the evening and the morning"* (Surah 40:55). The *"Teach Yourself Islam"* book, the details of which are in the Bibliography, state of Muhammad:
"All his recorded words and actions reveal him as a man of great gentleness, kindness, humility, good humour and excellent common sense, who had a great love for animals and for all people, especially children."
Now it is reasonable that people should present their faith in the best honest light, but the above statement in the light of recorded Muslim history is sheer propaganda. Perhaps he did have some positive qualities, but, as Dave Hunt remarks:
"Arab historians candidly admit that, in contrast to Christ's perfect life, Muhammad lied, cheated, lusted, deceived, robbed and killed, and often did it all in the name of Allah."

It seems that this tradition lives on in many quarters.

2.4. MUHAMMAD THE PROPHET AND THE KORAN

There was a cave in the mountain of Jebel Nur (or Mount Hir – both names are given) near Mecca, where people sometimes went to pray or meditate; it was there that Muhammad is claimed to have had a number of encounters, some apparently visionary and others invisible, mainly with the angel Gabriel (or Jibril), but occasionally apparently with Allah himself. Muhammad experienced many traumatic symptoms, and it has been suggested that these were epileptic fits; however this cannot be confirmed, and it would be unwise to pursue this possibility with Muslims; there are better ways to demonstrate which religion is of God.

Now Gabriel is revealed in the Bible as a mighty holy angel, a highly authoritative figure. but never as an archangel, a title reserved for Michael, He is first mentioned in the book of Daniel, where he appears several times. Later, within the Holy Place in the Jerusalem Temple, he described himself to Zacharias, the officiating priest for the day, thus: *"I am Gabriel, that stand in the presence of God; and am sent to speak unto thee, and to shew thee these glad tidings"* (Lk 1:19). This was six centuries before the Koran was written. If the Koran agreed with the words of Gabriel, then there might possibly be grounds for considering the authenticity of the Koran testimony; but it does not. We will see more of the Bible's recorded words of Gabriel in Chapter 3.

However it would be difficult to argue that his 'revelation' was merely the thoughts of a human mind, however brilliant or gifted he may have been. Muhammad was instructed to record over a period of twenty three years, but with a number of breaks, the substance of these encounters, not all of which took place within the original cave; the text is supposed to have been given from the original in Heaven. The Koran should not be confused with the Hadiths, or collected sayings of Muhammad, which are more highly venerated by some Muslims than by others.

Sidney Collett records:
> "Its first transcript was, according to the Mohammedans, written from the beginning in rays of light by the finger of God upon a gigantic tablet resting upon the throne of the Almighty. A copy of it, in a book bound in white silk, jewels and gold, was brought down by Gabriel on a particular night called 'the night of power' in the month of Ramadan. It is the contents of this book which were revealed to Mohammed."

One cannot help but recall the claimed origins of the Book of Mormon.

Muhammad admits to having been illiterate; this is the common interpretation, borne out by Islamic history, of Surah 7:158: *"So believe in Allah and His Messenger, the unlettered prophet."* He claims to have been told to memorise and to repeat what he had heard in the cave and during other 'visitations'. The word 'Koran' is derived from the Arabic for the verb 'to recite'. Islamic historians record that, when Muhammad dictated these memorised texts for recording in writing, Abdollah Sarh, one of these scribes, made various suggestions to Muhammad for the improvement of the text of the Koran, and that these were initially accepted. Mohammad later had Sark killed; as Dave Hunt remarks, perhaps he knew too much! It was Caliph Uthman, who, in a monumental work, put together all the scraps of manuscripts, some of which were very small, in a single co-ordinated volume. These and many other facts which deny the popularly accepted version as being the original can be found in the preserved writings of early Muslim scholars and in museums and archives..

It would probably be fair to say that, for an illiterate man, he had a remarkable memory for what he had heard about the older Scriptures. But he was frequently muddled about timings and sequences, confusing, as we shall see in Chapter 3, the birth of Jesus Christ with the plight of Hagar when cast out by Sarah, under a palm tree, rather than with Joseph and the manger. He confused Potiphar from Pharaoh's court in the time of Joseph with Haman of the Persian court twelve hundred years later. Gabriel, as the messenger of God, would never have made such basic errors!

Arabic is the only language recognised as the true vehicle of Islamic knowledge: *"So, [O Muhammad], We have only made it [the Qu'ran] easy to your tongue [i.e. the Arabic language] that you may give good tidings thereby to the righteous and warn thereby a hostile people"* (Surah 19:97).

2.5. MUHAMMAD'S LIFE CONTINUED

Muhammad gave the name 'Islam', which means 'submission' (to the will of Allah), and therefore to his new set of beliefs and disciplines. Initially he taught Islam to his wife and a few friends, but fairly soon thereafter to others. He was condemnatory of the confused polytheistic practices centred at the Ka'aba, to the obvious disquiet of his tribal members who had profited from the sale and provision of services to pilgrims, and saw their livelihoods at risk in any new regime.

Because of the different calendars, given dates may appear to vary by a year from record to record. In 619 AD he claimed to have been taken on the back of some mythical beast in his celebrated 'Night of Ascent' to what was later claimed to be the Temple Mount in Jerusalem. As we shall at 5.1., the Jerusalem location seems to have been an example of Islamic revisionism. He is claimed to have been caught up to the throne of God either physically or spiritually – one can see the influence of some Bible knowledge here, perhaps striving to emulate Paul (II Cor 12:2) or John (Rev 4:1). He is said to have been taken to a point beyond which even the angel Jibril was not permitted, one of the many proofs that Jibril and Gabriel are not one and the same: Compare with the Bible: *"I am Gabriel, that stand in the presence of God"* (Lk 1:19). In Heaven he claims to have met with Jesus, Abraham, Moses "and other prophets" and to have received instructions about the future conduct of prayer for Muslims.

He was compelled to leave Mecca and eventually in 622 AD settled in Yathrib, which was soon to be renamed 'Medina' (the town of the Prophet), some 250 miles to the north west, where he was well received. His move to Yathrib and extended stay there is termed the *'Hegira', Hejira'* or 'Hijra'. In Medina he eventually became the political as well as the religious leader, setting a precedent for numerous similar joint offices down through Islamic history.

During this absence from Mecca his followers grew in number. At first Christians and Jews were impressed by his monotheistic opposition to idolatry, and the earlier parts of the Koran are more well-disposed to these than the later parts, written when his new faith began to be rejected by them. He classed these as *ahl al-kitab* – 'people of the book', who had their own Scriptures. However, soon he expected to be heralded as the new Messiah, and, as these claims conformed neither to Old nor to New Testament prophecies, particularly as his descent was claimed from Ishmael and not David, they were soon rejected, attracting his enmity. However stubborn about other matters the Jews were, they had no doubts about this matter: *"While the Pharisees were gathered together, Jesus asked them, Saying, What think ye of Christ? whose son is he? They say unto him, The Son of David"* (Matt 22:41-42). Muhammad was no son of David. During his first year at Medina he observed the Jewish Day of Atonement (*Yom Kippur*) feast, but a year later he substituted that with the fasting month of Ramadan, which has remained a standard practice ever since. At Medina he demanded that the Jews in the city should convert to Islam; when they refused, he evicted them from their homes and pillaged their property. The Jews at nearby Khaybar were the first to have imposed upon them *dhimmi*, a tax, still levied in some Islamic countries upon non-Muslims – thus it was Muhammad himself who set a precedent for cashing in on the convictions of others who could not submit to what their own faith considered blasphemous. Anti-Semitism within Islam had begun, though down through the centuries it was not always pursued with such vigour or ferocity as it was then and is today.

Muhammad's change of attitude as Jews and Christians rejected his claims and as both his bitterness and confidence grew, is reflected by comparison of the earlier 2nd Surah with the later 9th. Islamic propagandists love to quote the former but not the latter: *"There shall be no compulsion in [acceptance of] the religion"* (2:256) ; this is interpreted as being no compulsion to convert. Contrast this with: *"And when the sacred months have passed, then kill the polytheists wherever you find them and capture them and besiege them and sit in wait for them at every place of ambush."* Surah 9.5. We see a little more of this at Section 3.3. Polytheism in Muhammad's mind included Christians, who are Trinitarian. Jews he recognised as being monotheistic, but were fair game for murder by the time Surah 9:29 was written.

To what extent his early followers were motivated by the new religion with its practices, and to what extent by the appeal of the booty, from what was suddenly claimed to be lawful raiding and warfare, would be impossible to say. At any rate, from Medina he led numerous unprovoked murderous attacks on caravans trading with Mecca, and even on other tribes and cities.

By 630 Muhammad, after two tentative visits during the previous two years, was strong enough to return to Mecca in triumph as the 'last and greatest of the prophets' and establish the Ka'aba, which he rid of its images and idols, as the central shrine of Islam, which it has remained ever since. Mecca replaced Jerusalem as a place towards which to pray.

Muhammad died in Mecca on the 8th of June 632 AD, survived by a number of wives and concubines. He had not appointed a successor as such, and soon two main factions developed, the large Sunni majority and a sizeable Shiah or Shi-ite minority. Muhammad's successor, considered a Sunni, quickly set off on a military campaign, slaying all who would not accept or submit to Islam. Muhammad's son-in-law. Ali, also known as Asadullah, who had married his favourite daughter, Fatima, and who claimed

A Brief History of Islam

to be Muhammad's successor, was assassinated; he is still venerated and his tomb visited by Shiahs or Shi'ites. Only in Iran and some areas close to its borders do Shias currently form a majority. Shiahs have, down through the centuries, split into a number of complex factions, whereas the Sunnis are divided here and there only by their differing levels of individual and collective commitment - or fanaticism. These two main parties may have some future significance in Ezekiel's prophecies, as we shall see in Chapter 7.7. Other groups which have emerged over the centuries include Barelvis, Deobandis, Isma'ilis, Jamaaitis, Naqshbandis, Salafis, Sufis, Wahabists, etc, almost comparable in number to Christian denominations and cults. We have no room to criticise there!

2.6. THE SPREAD OF ISLAM

During Muhammad's lifetime the south-western half of the Arabian Peninsula, from the Gulf of Aqaba to Aden, came under Islamic control, as did Oman on the far side of the desert. Following his death in 632 AD, Caliphs succeeded as leaders of Islam, exercising a mix of religious, political and military roles. Under Caliph Abu Bakir (632-634 AD) Islam spread over the rest of the Arabian Peninsula as far as Damascus and along the North African coast as far as Tripoli. During the ten following years, under Caliph Umar Ibn Al-Maliq, it spread westwards along the Mediterranean seaboard of Africa and northwards to cover Syria and Mesopotamia. In 638 AD Caliph Umar captured Jerusalem, which only nine years before had been recaptured from the Persians, who had devastated the city and destroyed many churches in 614 AD. Over the next few decades Islamic rule covered almost the entire area from the east end of the Black Sea to the river Indus, where it halted for several centuries, and also into Central Asia as far as Kabul.

For the first century of Islamic conquest there was limited pressure to convert, depending who was in command; sometimes Christian and Jewish communities were respected in accordance with certain earlier statements in the Koran. The resumption of pressure to convert to Islam on pain of death, while not totally unprecedented, is a comparatively, modern phenomenon. Admittedly non-Muslims in many Islamic countries were considered to be second class citizens with reduced rights, subject to special taxes. These things varied greatly from country to country and from century to century.

In 712 AD Islamic armies crossed the Straits of Gibraltar and conquered most of the Iberian Peninsula, less the Cantabrian and Western Pyrenees Mountains, advancing into south central France. They suffered a major defeat at the Battle of Poitiers in 732 AD, and withdrew to Spain, where a separate and powerful Caliphate, rivalling some of the Eastern ones, was established at Cordoba in the 10th Century, a development of the Umayyad Caliphate. The grand buildings of this period are now popular tourist attractions.

East of the Indus the Indian sub-continent was partly Islamised during the 14th Century, much becoming part of the Mughal (or Mogul) Empire before the arrival of European traders and colonists; Hinduism remained the majority religion and was generally tolerated. Islam then spread gradually, mainly through traders to the Malay Peninsula and many of the East Indies islands and as far as the south Philippines. Expansion was by no means always aggressive, especially when Islam was still a minority faith.

The nominally Christian Greek speaking Byzantine Empire held out against Islam for many centuries until the Islamic Ottoman conquest of Constantinople in 1455 AD, after which most of the Balkan lands of Bulgaria, Macedonia, Serbia and Thrace were invaded, and were becoming a bitterly fought frontier between Christianity and Islam, with areas like Hungary and Transylvania resisting fiercely, and others like Albania and Bosnia succumbing.

2.7. CHRISTIAN COUNTER ATTACKS
The Crusades of the 11th to 13th Centuries, which have long

been romanticised by historians, were an initiative of Pope Urban II. The avowed aim of the Crusaders was to recapture for Christendom (not, please note, for Israel) the holy sites in the Middle East. Superficially this may seem laudable enough, and one cannot doubt the sincerity and bravery of many of the Crusaders. However it did not take into consideration latter day prophecy regarding Israel and Jerusalem, and in no way conformed to God's revealed plans. Persecution of Jews in the homelands of some of the Crusaders was rife during this period. Unfortunately participation was presented as a means of grace for sinful kings, nobles, knights and others – salvation was thought to be more or less assured. This had no basis whatsoever in Biblical Christianity, and, indeed, can be compared to the lie currently fed to Jihadist martyrs that they will be rewarded for their deaths by quick entry into a carnal paradise with a multitude of maidens awaiting them.

In 1099 Baldwin of Bouillon captured and occupied Jerusalem, turning the mosques on the Temple Mount into cathedrals, in the same way as the cathedral of St Sophia in Constantinople later became the Blue Mosque. The Crusaders were trying to pre-empt end-time events. Noble feats were performed and atrocities perpetrated on both sides; the Muslim leader, Saladin, gained a reputation for chivalry equal to that of the most valiant Crusaders. The reconquest in 1187 AD of Jerusalem by Saladin was a huge blow. It should be noted that it was Saladin, not the Crusaders, who encouraged Jews to settle in Jerusalem! Such atrocities as were committed by Crusaders almost a thousand years ago, when opposing armies were fairly evenly matched, are still remembered as an insult against Islam, whereas the genocide or holocaust by the Ottomans of around a million and a half Christian Armenians in Anatolia in 1915, only a hundred years ago, when the attention of the world was on war elsewhere, is conveniently dismissed and denied by Muslim powers, and particularly by Turkey, the direct successors to the Ottomans. We return to this shortly. Muslims should consider that nobody insults Muhammad and Islam more than Muslims themselves by their behaviour.

Israel, The Church and Islam

The Christian *Reconquista* of Spain left the ever diminishing Caliphate of Granada (1248-1492) as the only remaining Muslim presence in Western Europe, Sicily having been retaken in 1130 AD. Such influence as Islam had in Europe during and after the Dark Ages was through their maintenance and development in Cairo University and elsewhere of the unique learning which the Greeks had founded in the fields of medicine, mathematics, philosophy and even astronomy, which learned men in the West were keen to acquire.

In 1538 the Ottoman Sultan, Suleiman the Magnificent, built the walls of Jerusalem which still stand. When he heard that Israel's Messiah is due to return via the Eastern Gate (Ezek 43:2,4), in blasphemous arrogance he had it sealed off. One day the same Suleiman, naked of his power, with his magnificence abandoned in the grave, will have to appear before the Lord Jesus Christ.

During the 18th Century there were great Christian revivals in Britain and America, seeking to restore some of the outreach of the early Church; many were saved. Within Islam that century there was a revival which sought to restore the former Jihadism and submission of the Prophet's time; many were slain as a result. 'Abd Al Wahab founded what has become known as Wahabism. It caught on quickly among the Sunnis of Arabia, and especially with the Saud clan. During the 19th Century it was suppressed by the Ottoman Turks; but after they were defeated by the British and Allies it was given free rein, and the Saud of that time, a man with numerous children by numerous women, proclaimed himself king of a new state which he named after himself, Saudi Arabia. Almost immediately a vast oilfield was discovered, giving financial resources which have been used to build magnificent mosques around the world and to bankroll terrorism.

Soon Iran and other Islamic countries with oil were able to exert their influence, which often took the form of blackmailing oil-dependent industrialised lands to co-operate. According to

A Brief History of Islam

recent statistics, the West might be in a position to blackmail several of these countries in return! The world's reserves of fresh water are in danger of running out by 2030, and water is an even more vital commodity than oil. The Trumpets of Revelation 8 and Bowls of Wrath of Revelation 16 foretell a very scorched earth in the period between the Lord's Return **for His Church** and His return **to the World**. The world may dread 2030, but we expect our Saviour at any moment.

2.8.　MODERN ISLAMIC REASSERTION AND EXPANSION

At sections 5.6.and 5.7 some of the following facts will be repeated and elaborated, but only with reference to Jerusalem. During the age of European expansion any military spread of Islam was limited, and more or less contained in the Balkans, the Russians during the 1877-1878 Russo-Turkish War giving protection to formerly oppressed Christians. The 'Christian' Russian Empire colonised the khanates of Central Asia, but allowed Islam to remain unmolested. The Dutch colonised the bulk of the partly Islamic East Indies and, as the Ottoman Empire shrank, much of Islamic North Africa came under British, Italian and particularly French influence.

What we now call Turkey was at least nominally Christian before the Ottoman invasion. Armenia, whose church is actually older than Roman Catholicism, had been absorbed by the Ottomans in the 16th Century, and in 1894 to 1896, despite largely unheard appeals to the West, around 300,000 Christians were slaughtered. Nevertheless by 1900 Christians formed almost a third of the population of Turkey proper. By 1927 this had fallen to less than two percent. Earlier, by 1908, the Young Turks had assumed power, initially as an attempt at a constitutional monarchy. But soon this leadership was reduced to a dictatorial triumvirate nick-named the Three Pashas, ending a short-lived policy of toleration of other nationalities and religions. Their allies, Germany, supposedly Christian, did not interfere, being much more interested in extending their colonial ambitions toward the Persian Gulf, the gateway to the East, via their Berlin to Baghdad railway. The Turkish massacre of one and a half million Armenian Christians was like a dress rehearsal for Hitler's Holocaust of the Jews. A network of deportation control centres and stations was set up and four deportation concentration and annihilation centres were established. The most unspeakable atrocities and cruelties were perpetrated against women, children and the infirm, few surviving the forced marches. Nearly all the Armenian able-bodied men were slaughtered. Hundreds of thousands of Assyrian Christians in the East and Greek Christians in the West were also massacred, although these, unlike the Armenians, were at least given the life-saving option of converting to Islam. Preparations for the centenary of the massacre are now afoot in Armenia, and elsewhere among descendants of those who fled to the United States and elsewhere.

Following World War I the League of Nations placed much of the formerly Ottoman Middle East under British and French mandate. Under the terms of the Balfour Declaration limited resettlement of Jews to the Promised Land took place, obviously against Islamic wishes and provoking resistance, particularly during 1936-39, despite the eagerness of absentee landlords to sell the land legally to the Jewish resettlers; records of such transactions still exist. We return to these matters at sections 5.7.and 5.8.

In 1924 Turkey publicly dissolved the Caliphate which most Muslims had regarded as the official representation of Allah upon earth. But it was an uneasy vacuum. The next serious modern Islamic assertion commenced with the March 1928 founding of the Muslim Brotherhood in Egypt as an Islamist religious, political and social movement. Thereafter there has been constant rivalry between secular and religious powers for control. The importance of crude oil to the world economy gave the area an importance which it had not enjoyed for many centuries. Where oil was absent, Nasser was able to use the critically important Suez Canal as a bargaining tool. During the Cold War Middle Eastern loyalties were divided between the Soviet Bloc and the West.

The Ayatolla Khomeini (1900-1989) described in the following words the aspirations of an ever widening cross section of Islamic society, helping to explain the current desire to impose Sharia Law wherever it can:

> "Islamic government is a government of divine law. The difference between Islamic government and constitutional government lies in the fact that, in the latter system, it is the representatives of the people or those of the king who legislate and make laws. Whereas the actual authority belongs to Allah. No others, no matter who they may be, have the right to legislate, nor has any person the right to govern on any basis other than the authority that has been conferred by Allah.... It is the religious expert and no one else who should occupy himself with the affairs of government."

Some of these 'religious experts' have been not only fanatical, but also murderous. Long ago it was 'religious experts' who handed Jesus Christ over to the authorities for crucifixion.

Were what we have just described to have been applied fairly, with equal stringency for men and women, without such draconian punishments for non-capital offences and not subject to the whims of individual clerics, which a normal judicial system would try to balance or eliminate, all this might have its merits compared with our increasingly secular Western administrations. Encouraged by militant secularism, these are now ever more stubbornly and deliberately rejecting the sanctions and moral codes derived from the Ten Commandments and other Biblical teaching, which for so long stood us in good stead. Those in Strasburg, London and now Edinburgh who defy God in such matters are, whether they believe it or not, ultimately answerable to their Creator. They bring comfort to Islam by allowing Muslims, as I mentioned in Chapter 1, to claim the higher moral ground.

From this it is not difficult to see the background of the recent 'Arab Spring'. Shariah Law is applied in Saudi Arabia to execute any person who converts to Christianity, and in Pakistan, for instance, for blaspheming Muhammad – a prophet, not God! Nobody is or has been more aware of the dangers to internal stability than some of the tough rulers of certain Islamic countries, whom the West has been naïve enough to see as impediments to aspirations for democracy. Pure Islam and democracy are utterly incompatible, for reasons given in the Ayatolla's statement quoted above. Saddam Hussein, Gaddafi, Mubarak and Assad are examples of rulers, whom we most certainly never uphold as paragons of virtue, who were aware of the even greater dangers to their non-Muslim minorities than those who wanted to oust them. At the time of writing only Assad survives, and the Mufti of Jerusalem has issued an edict promising Paradise to anyone who will assassinate him!

The Arab Spring started in fact with the spectacular self-incineration of a Tunisian fruit seller, Mohamed Bouazizi. In December 2010 his business and that of his fellow merchants had been rendered impossible by the corruption, bribery and general persecution by the minions of state officialdom. Aptly the torch thus lit spread like wildfire through Islamic countries with similar regimes; the forlorn hope was that 'pure' Islam would bring order and honesty. Instead, it has brought further chaos and terrorism, and some actually long for the bad old days, which were at least better than the even worse new days. In Tunisia where it started, Islamic State representatives announced that the murder of twenty-two foreign tourists was designed to destroy the tourist industry, one of the country's main sources of income. In Syria alone since the 'Spring' started in 2010 up till the beginning of 2015, 76,000 have been killed, a million homes have been partially or totally destroyed and around four million have become refugees; and this is what happens when Islam becomes more fundamental! The demise of the old regimes has left a power vacuum, to be filled with undisciplined mobs, who believe that the cry that "Allah is great!" – *Allahu Aknar* - is sufficient to justify any carnage or barbarity.

The 'Islamic State' which is emerging, with splinter groups in

A Brief History of Islam

many lands, has yet to take on a final form. It claims to be the restored Caliphate, representing Allah upon earth. The al-Shabaab of East Africa, led by Mohamed Mohamud, is now trying to compete with the Syrian-Iraqi Isis in the level of slaughter and deportation of non-Muslims. But an ineffective Western world is more pre-occupied with admittedly important matters such as general elections, presidential elections and economics. Political commentator Ross Clark in April 2015 wrote:

> "The trouble is too many of our politicians seem frightened of extremist Islam. They avoid any kind of confrontation for fear of stoking antipathy, even to the point of declaring – preposterously – that IS, Boko Haram, Al-Shabaab have 'nothing to do with Islam'."

Leaders are responsible to their Creator for the stewardship of their appointments. Church leaders are also responsible. Appropriately, in their Easter messages, the Pope and the Archbishop of Canterbury, whilst deploring the recent massacres of Christians and appropriately indicating that the Christian response should not be a violent one, inappropriately omitted to take the golden opportunity to point out that the Christians' God will hold the perpetrators responsible if they do not repent. There is nothing loving in failing to warn people of fearful consequences.

Within the Islamic State recruits have been required to participate or at least watch beheadings as part of their initiation process. Where Christians refuse to renounce their Christianity and to face death, their executioners perversely are helping to bring eternal blessing upon their victims: *"If any man serve me, him will my Father honour"* (Jn 12:26); *"Others were tortured, not accepting deliverance; that they might obtain a better resurrection"* (Heb 11:35); *"Be thou faithful unto death, and I will give thee a crown of life"* (Rev 2:10). And as for the executioners? Well, let us remember that Paul, the greatest Christian missionary of all, had been an approving bystander at Stephen's martyrdom. One can always hope and pray.

Things happen so quickly within the Islamic world, and especially where it interfaces with other faiths, that it would be of limited value to bring this brief history completely up-to-date. The situation changes almost daily. We turn now to the topic of Islamic theology. The claims of descent of Islam from Abraham and earlier will be covered in Chapter 4, because ancient prophecies, true and false, are important, and much foreshadowed in the Scriptures is now coming into sharper focus.

Several hundred years ago it was widely accepted within Islam that Muslims could declare other Muslims infidels and so murder them with impunity. Shortly before the Arab Spring it was calculated by a leading authority that at least twelve million Muslims had already perished this way. One wonders how many more have since died and how many are still to do so.

CHAPTER THREE

The Theology of Islam

*I am Jehovah, that is my name; and my glory
will I not give to another*
(Isa 42:8 Dby)

3. 1. THE KORAN AND HADITHS

In the previous chapter we looked at how the Koran came to be written. Although the word 'Theology' is often more widely interpreted, its true meaning is the study or knowledge of God, and I propose to limit this chapter largely to that, and to a brief comparison of the contrasting doctrines of salvation, and leave other doctrines until we encounter them in later chapters. Within the Koran, the term Surah (or Sura) indicates something about mid-way between the books and the chapters of the Bible. There are 114 Surahs in all. Sometimes one encounters long chains of extremely short verses, and then remarkably long ones. As a book, it contains much scolding rhetoric about Judaism and Christianity, compared to the Bible's smaller but more reasoned proportion of condemnation of false doctrine. Strictly speaking, the plural of hadith is *ahadith*, but 'hadiths' seems to be better understood by non-Muislims; the term will be explained shortly.

We can contend more effectively for our own faith if we are aware of the basic tenets of those to whom we are witnessing, particularly those tenets which relate to the God (or god) whom we or they worship. With Islam, the theology and other tenets of faith are contained in the Koran. The Koran is a comparatively short book, comparable in length to the New Testament. It has 6,666 verses – a statistic to be pondered over, but not to be dogmatic about, when one thinks of the 666 of Rev 13:8. It is not an easy book to read and reflects what, to Western culture at least, is a strange mind set.

Muhammad seems to have been well aware of the Torah (the five books of the Law) and the Psalms, but much less aware of the remainder of the Tanakh or Old Testament. Muhammad denied that the Torah, which has existed for well over three thousand years, was the original given by Allah to Moses. Well, we would say 'Amen' to that, because Allah had nothing to do with it. The content of those five books did not support Islam, so in ten different Surahs Muhammad denounced its authenticity as it has been known for over two thousand years. Also he was clearly aware of the four Gospels, but evidently not so much of the remainder of the New Testament. While he did not denounce the authenticity of the Gospels in the way that he did the Old Testament, his revision of New Testament **teaching** was more extensive than that of such Old Testament teaching of which he had been aware. The Koran acknowledges the evil personality of Pharaoh, the crossing of the Red Sea and some of the miracles that followed. But, compared to the straightforward sequential historical record of the Old Testament books up to II Chronicles, such OT episodes as one encounters in the Koran are an incredible muddle.

What astonishes many Christians when they first open the Koran, and I include myself as one of the astonished, is how superficially like the Bible much of it is, although the sequence of dealing with historical events recorded in the Bible is weird. But then one quickly comes to see how much of it is a parody of Bible teaching rather than a parallel book. It cannot logically be claimed, though illogically it often is, that any differences between the Bible and the Koran regarding the same topic must be corruptions of the Biblical original, the Koran being the revision or correction. There is a vast amount of direct and

The Theology of Islam

indirect manuscript evidence which pre-date Muhammad. The 2nd Century BC Septuagint Alexandrian Greek translation of the Old Testament is frequently quoted in the Gospels, including by Jesus Christ Himself. However even such overwhelming academic proof of the greater antiquity of the Bible, is not guaranteed to enhance what should be spiritual discussion. Muhammad is thought by Muslims to have been deceived by Satan at one point, resulting in the famous 'Satanic verses', so publicised in Salman Rushti's controversial book. These verses have now been deleted from the Koran. There is nothing comparable with these in the Bible; *"All scripture is given by inspiration of God"* (II Tim 3:16).

The Koran, while overtly recognising much in general of Christianity, actually contains many direct attacks on the fundamental Christian truths, such as the Trinity, the Deity of Christ, the death of Christ, the means of salvation and God's declared purposes for Israel etc, thus legitimising in the minds of some Muslims, physical attacks upon Christians and Jews, even if a great many have no wish to get involved personally. When we consider some of the more subtle differences between the two faiths, we might be reminded of the *"Hath God said?" opening* gambit of the Serpent in Gen 3:3, as opposed to a direct denial, or of the Lk 4:10-11 inappropriate use by Satan of genuine Scripture during our Lord's wilderness temptations to manipulate for sinister purposes.

The Hadiths, or Traditions, revered by Muslims only second to the Koran, are a collection of non-Koranic teachings associated with Muhammad. The main Sunni and Shiah written versions, which date from the 9th Century differ, but not significantly. Some sayings are accorded more reliability than others, those which agree with other Hadith entries being given the higher reliability, *sahih* being sound, *hasan* fairly reliable and *da'if*, weak. Islamic teachers have over many years produced from the Koran and Hadiths the immensely complex Shariah Law, which governs almost every conceivable aspect of the Muslim's life. In some ways this is reminiscent of the sterile religion of the Pharisees which Jesus so strongly condemned: *"Then the Pharisees and scribes asked him, Why walk not thy disciples according to the tradition of the elders, but eat bread with unwashen hands? He answered and said unto them, Well hath Esaias prophesied of you hypocrites, as it is written, This people honoureth me with their lips, but their heart is far from me. Howbeit in vain do they worship me, teaching for doctrines the commandments of men..... And he said unto them, Full well ye reject the commandment of God, that ye may keep your own tradition"* (Mk 7:5-9).

3.2. THE BIBLE PRE-DATES THE KORAN

The canon of what we regard as Holy Scripture was complete by the end of the 1st Century, even though widespread consolidation was not reached for around another couple of hundred years. Certain small Eastern fringe churches, were not party to such agreement and have long preserved minor differences, particularly in the sequence of the epistles. Also the Roman Catholic Church incorporates the Old Testament Apocrypha, which is never quoted in the New Testament and was regarded as inspired neither by the Apostles nor by Orthodox Jews. The sixty-six books which we recognise as the Holy Scriptures, are the only authoritative basis for presenting Christianity to Muslims. Many Muslim scholars will tacitly accept this as being authoritative, **except** when the Koran disagrees – which is frequently!

Over the seven months during which I have been writing this book and peering regularly into the Koran, I have become more and more convinced that, while the personality of Muhammad, the Prophet of Islam, shines through the pages of the Koran, it is impossible to believe that there is no inhuman hand behind this strange volume, such are the subtleties of the underlying denials of, among other truths, that fundamental central truth regarding *"The holy scriptures, which are able to make thee **wise unto salvation through faith which is in Christ Jesus**"* (II Tim 3:15). Paul warned the Galatians: *"But though we, or an* *angel from heaven, preach any other gospel unto you than that which we have preached unto you, let him be accursed"* (Gal 1:8). Jibril is not to be trusted! Muhammad's confusion over the Jewish and Christian Scriptures which he claimed to respect, testifies to human fallibility; but that should not be allowed to cloud the central issue of the strange power behind the book.

3.3. GOD AND ALLAH ARE NOT THE SAME
The importance of understanding this distinction simply cannot be over-emphasised. Whatever syncretistic and ecumenical school governors teach to the contrary, **we do not all worship the same deity**. The differences are fundamental in the extreme. Our calling God 'Allah' would be blasphemy. It would be like Elijah addressing Jehovah as 'Baal', rather than making the emphatic distinction between them that he did.

Around eleven hundred years before Muhammad, *"Ezra blessed **Jehovah, the great God**; and all the people answered, Amen, Amen! with lifting up of their hands; and they bowed their heads, and worshipped Jehovah with their faces to the ground"* (Neh 8:5-6 Dby). Television news readers and newspaper editors sometimes report that atrocities have been committed by a person or persons shouting "God is great!". In fact they say no such thing. What in fact they say, usually in Arabic, is "Allah is great!" And that is entirely different. Vatican and other denominational spokesmen have given what is, when one thinks about it, blasphemous recognition that Allah is God or another name for God. The implications of such false claims are immense. The Koran itself recognises that Allah is a name, as opposed to a title or designation. In the opening Surah one reads, *"Allah is a proper **name** belonging only to the one Almighty God, Creator and Sustainer of the heavens and earth and all that is within them, the Eternal and Absolute, to whom alone all worship is due"* (Surah 1:2). Let us comment:-
- Unlike the literature of various Oriental religions, one can immediately see how the Koran has been written by someone reasonably familiar with our Bible.

- Allah is a name; therefore *if* we must compare Allah with names in our theology, we should do so with 'Jehovah' or 'Yahweh', and not with 'God'. The Bible tells us: *"And God spoke to Moses, and said to him, I am Jehovah. And I appeared unto Abraham, unto Isaac, and unto Jacob, as the Almighty God; but by my **name** Jehovah I was not made known to them"* (Ex 6:2-3 Dby). God told Moses to use that name when demanding that Pharaoh should let His people go, and ordered that it was to be taught to the children. Many translations substitute LORD in small block capitals for Jehovah in the Old Testament, and the Greek *Kurios* in the New Testament. As in the Septuagint, the Greek translation quoted in the New Testament. Jehovah, or Yahweh are pronounceable versions of the YHWH, the Hebrew tetragram which has no vowels. *"I am Jehovah, **that is my name**; and my glory will I not give to another, neither my praise unto graven image"* (Isa 42:8 ASV). For serious discussions with Muslims the Darby and the old American Standard versions with their unsubstituted names could be advantageous.
- The Bible states that the name of the One who created the Heavens is Jehovah: *"For all the gods of the peoples are idols: But Jehovah made the heavens"*. (I Chron 16:26 Dby); *"Thou art Jehovah, even thou alone; thou hast made heaven, the heaven of heavens, with all their host, the earth and all things that are thereon, the seas and all that is in them, and thou preservest them all"* (Neh 9:6 ASV). As quoted above, the Koran claims that Allah is *"the one Almighty God, Creator and Sustainer of the heavens and earth"* (Surah 1:2). Whoever this Jibril, who dictated this to Muhammad, was, he must have been fully aware that such statements are a perversion of Holy Scriptures, **ascribing to Allah the attributes of Jehovah**.
- Allah is said to be unknowable. Our God is knowable: *"And I will give them an heart to know me, that I am the*

The Theology of Islam

> *LORD: and they shall be my people, and I will be their God: for they shall return unto me with their whole heart"* (Jer 24:7); *"And this is life eternal, that they might know thee the only true God, and Jesus Christ, whom thou hast sent"* (Jn 17:3).

- Muslims, in their interpretation of submission, are unable to negotiate reverently with Allah, resulting in a fatalistic Kismet philosophy (Turkish derived from Arabic *qisma*). Abraham, the *'friend of God'* (II Chron 20:7, Jas 2:23) could negotiate for Sodom (Gen 18:22-23), knowing that God would listen before acting; Moses did the same to avert judgment (Ex 32:11-13). As Christian believers we are called friends (Jn 15:14), and have the right and duty to intercede even for the unworthy. Allah never calls his people friends and many Muslims seem to take delight in executing those they consider unworthy, I repeat: *"Kill the polytheists wherever you find them and capture them and besiege them and sit in wait for them at every place of ambush"* (Surah 9:5); *"fight those who do not believe in Allah"* (9:29).

The Old Testament refers by name to numerous heathen gods. Many were developed from deities worshipped as far back as Nimrod and the Tower of Babel, and may even have been reintroduced from the Antediluvian world by Ham after the Flood. Fallen angelic powers behind some of the previously worshipped gods, being fallen spirits and not mortal, had not been destroyed by the Flood waters, although many of the most evil had been incarcerated in the Abyss (I Pet 3:19-20, Rev 9:2 etc). The Tower, which God destroyed, had been a ziggurat or astrological observatory. Any serious study is highly complex and quite unnecessary for our needs, but so many of these demi-gods can be traced back to the worship of various heavenly bodies. Some gained new names after the dispersal from Babel, as they spread through different tribes and nations. Such devolved names as Baal and Chemosh will be familiar to readers of the Old Testament.

3.4. THE MOON GOD

We noted in Chapter 2 that the Ka'aba had numerous gods, many no doubt originating from this ancient panoply. Allah is a contraction of the name 'al Ihah', the important moon god, which Muhammad chose to honour from among the many others. Following Babel, veneration of the moon god, variously known as the 'Man of the Moon', Mother-Night, Deus Lunus etc., spread far and wide. In his great reform, King Josiah purged the land of moon worship: *"And he put down the idolatrous priests, whom the kings of Judah had ordained to burn incense in the high places in the cities of Judah, and in the places round about Jerusalem; them also that burned incense unto Baal, to the sun, and to the moon, and to the planets, and to all the host of heaven"* (II Kings 23:5). Next to the sun, which was particularly revered in Egypt, for instance, the moon was considered a most important deity, as the 'Numberer' or powerful controller of the times and tides. The lunar emblems themselves were ancient: *"So Gideon arose and killed Zebah and Zalmunna, and took the crescent ornaments that were on their camels' necks"* (Judg 8:21 NKJV). When in July 1948 the newly independent Islamic state of Pakistan was founded, an elaborate set of magnificent postage stamps was issued, with a crescent moon facing the right. Somebody spotted that this, at least in the local tradition, was insulting to Allah, because, according to them, the moon should have faced the left. By February 1949 a redrawn set was issued. I have both sets! Today the moon as an emblem on the top of mosques is at least as common as a cross on churches.

Worship of the moon may be identified in certain old Scandinavian, Saxon and Celtic festivals, which have been absorbed in vaguely modified forms into our questionable 'Christian' calendar. Jews, before the Captivity, seem to have incorporated some moon worship along with other pagan idolatry: *"But ye who forsake Jehovah, who forget my holy mountain, who prepare a table for Gad, and fill up mixed wine unto Meni":* (Isa 65:11 Dby). It is thought that Meni here was one name for the moon god.

The Theology of Islam

Yes, Muhammad did discard a whole panoply of ancient gods of the Ka'abah, but, as we have just seen, he kept one, which is no more acceptable for Christians to worship and venerate, than any other of that brood. Muslims consider any insult to Allah a capital offence, and in recent times have applied this rigorously in some lands. Christians tend to regard blasphemy more lightly, believing that individuals are directly answerable to God, who alone is entitled to take vengeance: *"Vengeance belongeth unto me, I will recompense, saith the Lord"* (Heb 10:30). He does not need our help in this serious matter. However we, at the opposite extreme, tend to be far too casual, and this brings Christianity to shame in the eyes of Muslims. But the fact remains that the god whom Muslims worship, however sincerely, is not our God. Paul writes: *"The things which the Gentiles sacrifice they sacrifice to demons and not to God, and I do not want you to have fellowship with demons"* (I Cor 10:20 NKJV). I use the NKJV here, because the KJV talks of 'devils', rather than 'demons'; only one Devil is spoken of in the Bible – Satan.

3.5. THE HOLY TRINITY

Muslims, like Orthodox Jews and some of the cults, lay great emphasis on the fact that they are monotheistic, believing in and worshipping one God. We Christians are likewise monotheistic, but, as we will see in the next two sections, Muslims find it difficult to understand how this can be so, as we worship Jesus Christ as well as God the Father. We approach the Father in the Name of and through the merits of the Lord Jesus Christ, as enabled by the Holy Spirit.

We dare not try to *expound* the Holy Trinity; to attempt to do so would be to suggest that we finite beings can understand the One Who created and controls the universe, and yet *"is not far from every one of us: for in him we live, and move, and have our being"* (Acts 17:27-28). We may not *understand* this, but we can *accept* it, and, having accepted it, we have the witness of the Holy Spirit dwelling within us to know that it is true. Our attitude should be like that of the overawed seraphim seen in vision by Isaiah (6:2-3), and the twenty-four elders in Rev 4:10-11.

However, in dealing with Islam, we have no alternative but to try to explain what we understand by the Holy Trinity, because Muslims see Christians, being Trinitarian, as having three Gods. To us it is elementary that this is NOT what we claim; but to them it is an enigma. Because Muhammad could not or would not accept the doctrine of the Holy Trinity, he had the unbelievable effrontery to deny it as a truth, and, worse, to lead fifty succeeding generations of his followers not to accept it.

The Koran affirms in Surah 4:171 that Allah is not a trinity, saying that Jesus is a mere messenger in contrast to Allah: *"The Messiah, Jesus, the son of Mary, was but a messenger of Allah and His word which He directed to Mary and a soul [created at a command] from Him. So believe in Allah and His messenger. And do not say 'Three', desist – it is better for you, indeed, Allah is but one God."* Muhammad simply did not understand the 'Three' of the Holy Trinity. Trinitarianism in Islam is known as *shirk*, and is considered a grave offence. Moreover the Koran teaches that Jesus was a created Being. The Bible, in contrast, had earlier declared: *"In the beginning was the Word, and the Word was with God, and the Word was God. The same was in the beginning with God. All things were made by him; and without him was not anything made that was made"* (Jn 1:1-3); *"For by him were all things created, that are in heaven, and that are in earth, visible and invisible, whether they be thrones, or dominions, or principalities, or powers: all things were created by him, and for him"* (Col 1:16); *"God, who at sundry times and in divers manners spake in time past unto the fathers by the prophets, Hath in these last days spoken unto us by his Son, whom he hath appointed heir of all things, **by whom also he made the worlds"*** (Heb 1:1-2). Ascribing deity to Jesus Christ is regarded by Muslims as a heinous offence. It is essential that we should be able to explain simply the basis of our faith in this core matter.

The Theology of Islam

Muhammad vilifies us, because to him it was blasphemy - the placing of Jesus Christ (or anyone else) on the same level as the one he sees as being God: *"Allah does not forgive association with Him, but He forgives what is that for whom He wills. And he who associates others with Allah has certainly fabricated a tremendous sin"* (Surah 4:48).

We are privileged to eavesdrop on a conversation within the Holy Trinity: *"And God said, Let us make man in our image, after our likeness"* (Gen 1:26). Jesus, before His arrest and crucifixion, prayed, referring to a situation which had existed thousands of years before Mary was born: *"And now, O Father, glorify thou me with thine own self with the glory which I had with thee before the world was"* (John 17:5). Some other privileged insights into conversations within the Godhead are to be found in Genesis 1:26, 3:22, 11:7, Psalm 2, Isaiah 6:8 and that sublime first chapter of Hebrews. Islam is unaware of these truths.

At His incarnation, *"The Word was made flesh, and dwelt among us, (and we beheld his glory, the glory as of the only begotten of the Father) full of grace and truth* (Jn 1:14)? **Jesus did not cease to be God when voluntarily His *situation* and *circumstances* changed when He became Man,** but He remained Who He had always been. Few passages are more succinct and easily expounded step by step to others than Phil 2:5-8; back at Section 1.2. we saw how the same passage illustrates the contrasts between Islam and Christianity: *"Let this mind be in you which was also in Christ Jesus, who, being in the form of God, did not consider it robbery to be equal with God, but made Himself of no reputation, taking the form of a bondservant, and coming in the likeness of men. And being found in appearance as a man, He humbled Himself and became obedient to the point of death, even the death of the cross"* (NKJV). Further confirmation of His continuing Divinity whilst "veiled in flesh" is found in the fact that throughout His life on earth the Holy Spirit was in constant communication with the Son.

Muslims think of Jews as being monotheistic because the vast majority of Jews do not teach the Holy Trinity, whereas most Christians do. Most Jews would agree with Muslims with this perception. However, as Tony Pearce of *Light for the Last Days* writes:

> It is interesting how many indications there are in the Hebrew Bible and in Jewish writings pointing to God being a plural unity, as Christians understand Him to be in the Persons of the Father, Son and Holy Spirit. In Jewish writing there is the idea of *the 'Memra'*, Aramaic for *'the Word'* (the expression used in John 1 for the incarnation of the Lord Jesus).."

We might add: *"Who is the image of the invisible God, the firstborn of every creature"* (Col 1:15); *"For in him dwelleth all the fulness of the Godhead bodily"* (Col 2:9). The Christian Jewish scholar, David Baron, speaks of this theme at greater length, concluding with the fact that the Voice from the burning bush said: *"I am the God of thy father, the God of Abraham, the God of Isaac, and the God of Jacob. And Moses hid his face; for he was afraid to look upon God"* (Ex 3:6). The AV: *"Hear, O Israel: The LORD our God is one LORD"* (Deut 6:4) is better rendered, especially when talking to Jews or Muslims: *"Hear, O Israel: Jehovah our God is one Jehovah,"* but it can also be translated: *"Jehovah is our God, Jehovah alone"*. As three Gospel writers record, Jesus referred to this as part of the greatest commandment (Matt 12:29, Lk 10:27-28 etc). In fact the monotheism of the Old Testament, though less easy to perceive, is exactly the same monotheism as the New Testament doctrine of the Holy Trinity. Ponder that! It is Islam which is 'out on a limb' here, not Christianity.

Not once in the Koran is Allah referred to as a father or *Abb*, further confirmation, were it needed, that he is not our God. Allah is sometimes referred to as *Rabb*, which in some English translations of the Koran is rendered 'Lord'.

3.6. ISLAMIC UNDERSTANDING OF THE BIRTH OF JESUS CHRIST

The Christian understanding, which is very different from the

The Theology of Islam

Islamic, is derived from such passages as Lk 1:31-32. It was Gabriel who said to Mary: *"And, behold, thou shalt conceive in thy womb, and bring forth a son, and shalt call his name JESUS. He shall be great, and shall be called **the Son of the Highest:** and the Lord God shall give unto him the throne of his father David: And he shall reign over the house of Jacob for ever; and of his kingdom there shall be no end"*. Gabriel went on to explain to Mary: *"**The Holy Ghost** shall come upon thee, and the **power of the Highest** shall overshadow thee: therefore also that holy thing which shall be born of thee shall be called the Son of God"* (v 35). **The whole Godhead was involved**.

No greater proof is required to prove that Muhammad's messenger, angelic or otherwise, was not the same as the one sent to Zacharias and Mary, because, while Muslims acknowledge that Christ's birth was miraculous, in accordance with the Koran, they vehemently deny that Jesus is the Son of God, or indeed that God has a Son.

Although Islam so vigorously denies the deity and Sonship of Christ, it does recognise that His conception and birth were miraculous and unique. The 19th Surah is entitled 'Surah Maryam'. There is also much in Surah 3, starting at v 36. Mary, that lovely, humble maiden whose virgin status is shown in the Gospels to have ended after Jesus' birth, who acknowledged *"God my Saviour"*, thus invalidating any spurious claims of her own "immaculate conception", and whom the New Testament is careful to give no prominence after Christ's Ascension, had, by the time Muhammad was around, gained within an increasingly apostate Church a status which would have horrified Mary herself, had she not, like all other believers, still been awaiting a future resurrection.

Muhammad almost certainly encountered some who called themselves Christians who worshiped the Virgin Mary. He can hardly be blamed for having assumed this to be orthodox (with a small 'o') Christianity. The Coptic and Nestorian churches, like the Roman Church in the West, had by the 7th Century absorbed much from paganism. Part of the Coptic tradition had been declared heretical in some of its teaching by the 5th Century Council of Chalcedon, and Nestorianism was condemned by the Council of Ephesus. It became a common, though not universal, assumption on the Eastern fringe of 'Christendom', that Mary was the third Person of the Trinity!

A dominant pagan feature had been the idea of a Mother-god or Mother of God, something first encountered in the form of Semiramis, back in the time of Nimrod and the Tower of Babel. She periodically changed her name but not her nature as the newly polyglot Babel devotees dispersed to new homelands. In due course she began to be given such titles as the Queen of Heaven, so severely denounced by God in Jeremiah (eg 44:17-19), yet still used within the Roman Catholic Church today. In the Old Testament she is sometimes seen as Ashteroth, the wife of El and mother of Baal, with carved pillars, probably a bit like totem poles, erected on hill tops in her honour. Mary was, of course, the **mother of our Lord's humanity, not His divinity**. The spread throughout the ancient world of the cult of the Madonna and Child is thoroughly researched in Hislop's classic, *"The Two Babylons"* (see Bibliography). When Islam is so divided, we need not be embarrassed about pointing out the divisions within what calls itself Christianity. In Mk 3:32-35 Jesus carefully detracted from any idea that Mary had any authoritative spiritual role, concluding with the words: *"For whosoever shall do the will of God, the same is my brother, and my sister, and mother."*

False teaching within Christianity plays into the hands of those Muslims who would discredit us. We may find it useful to emphasise that the Bible teaches that we should not and must not worship Mary. God declared: *"I am Jehovah, that is my name; and **my glory will I not give to another**, neither my praise to graven images"* (Isa 42:8 Dby). Mary is thus excluded by this statement, but the Lord Jesus Christ is not (Jn 17:5, Phil 2:9-11 etc); moreover the Name Jehovah is shown here,

The Theology of Islam

as in certain other passages, not limited within the Godhead to the Father. Angels are also excluded: *"And I John saw these things, and heard them. And when I had heard and seen, I fell down to worship before the feet of the angel which shewed me these things. Then saith he unto me, **See thou do it not**: for I am thy fellowservant, and of thy brethren the prophets, and of them which keep the sayings of this book: **worship God**"* (Rev 22:8-9). Those two verses are useful in contrasting to Muslims the Deity of Christ, Who is worshipped, not merely one of the prophets, of whose number Muhammed claimed to be. Those denominations who worship or pray to saints have much to answer for, in that they reinforce the Islamic idea that Christians are polytheistic. 'Canonisation' to 'sainthood' is utterly foreign to the Bible; the fact that all believers are saints, and that all dead saints irrespective of how godly their lives may have been, await the same resurrection, is a Bible truth.

3.7. THE DIVINE SONSHIP OF JESUS CHRIST

Within Islam Jesus is recognised as a prophet, but not as Prophet, Priest and King. We have already quoted Surah 19:30, purportedly spoken from the cradle; let us now complete the saying: *"[Jesus] said, 'Indeed I am the servant of Allah. He has given me the Scripture and made me a prophet'"*. In fact Jesus had not taken on His role as Prophet at this time; every subtle distortion is significant when examined.

Jesus – His name is always isolated from 'Christ' in the Koran – is recognised by Muslims as the Jewish Messiah sent to the twelve tribes – eventually to convert them to Islam! His teaching is respected in much the same way as it is among liberal 'Christians', who are quite happy to accept in a general, non-committal sort of way His Sermon on the Mount and His parables. They object strongly to anything He personally or New Testament writers say about Who He actually is.

If anything, the Christian claim that Christ is the Son of God is even more offensive to the Muslim than the associated doctrine

Israel, The Church and Islam

of the Holy Trinity. Muhammad could only think of sonship in biological terms, forgetting that human relationships are a mere shadow of the Divine, rather than that Divine relationships are the supreme state, of which we, who are made in God's image, are the minute and only partial copies. Muhammad's followers think of Christians as making the same incredibly dangerous false assumption. Surah 4:171 continues with the statement referring back to Allah, *"Exalted is He above having a son."* Islam thus affirms that their god has no son – again thinking of sonship in carnal terms.

For almost two thousand years Christians have accepted the miraculous incarnation without any need for God to resort to a physical relationship with Mary. This stems from a higher view of a God who does not have to be thought of in the most basic human terms. If Muslims want to know what Christians believe without going into detail - and it is very different – they could look at Christmas hymns in the average hymn book (not carol books which sometimes include 'Christianised' traditional pagan songs). Admittedly hymns are of course anything but infallible, but many capture Bible truths: "He came down to earth from Heaven, Who is God and Lord of all"; "Lo, within a manger lies, He who built the starry skies"; "Lo! He abhors not the virgin's womb; very God, begotten not created"; "Late in time, behold Him come, Offspring of a virgin's womb. Veiled in flesh the Godhead see, Hail the incarnate Deity, pleased as Man with man to dwell, Jesus our Emmanuel."

The fact that Allah has no son, which we do not dispute, is proclaimed in great letters round the dome of the Al Aqsar Mosque in Jerusalem, the city to which our Bible tells us that Christ will return in great glory (Zech 14:4) - the city outside the walls of which our Saviour prayed: "*Father, the hour is come; glorify thy Son, that thy Son also may glorify thee:* (Jn 17:1), the city within twenty miles of which *"there came a voice from heaven, saying, Thou art my beloved Son, in whom I am well pleased"* (Mk 1:11). The contrast between our God and Allah could therefore not be greater – a God who gave His Son and a god who has no son to give.

Our God's love is demonstrated in His having given His Son for a sinful world, e.g. Jn 3:16, Allah is said to be merciful, but not to sinners. *"Allah loves those who are constantly repentant and loves those who purify themselves"* (Surah 2:222). Compare with Rom 5:8: *"But God commendeth his love toward us, in that, while we were yet sinners, Christ died for us"*, a Christ who said: *"I came not to call the righteous, but sinners to repentance"* (Mk 2:17). Were Christians to show more often the joy (not mere emotion) of sins forgiven, our witness to Muslims would be so very much more effective. Many Muslims who have come to saving faith in Jesus Christ testify to the fact that they had been amazed to discover that God actually loves them; this had had a huge impact upon them.

We read that, when confronted by Jesus, demons whom He was casting out from possessed individuals had no option but to confess Jesus' Divine Sonship, something which at other times they would never have admitted: *"And unclean spirits, when they saw him, fell down before him, and cried, saying, Thou art the Son of God"* (Mk 3:11). One dreadful day all who have denied the Sonship of the Lord Jesus Christ, and in particular those who have taught others to do so, will, following the Second Resurrection, be finally confronted by *"Him that sat on* (the throne), *from whose face the earth and the heaven fled away"* (Rev 20:11). There will then be no hiding place; they will have no option but to make the same public confession as those unclean spirits of old.

3.8. THE KORAN AND THE 'INFANCY GOSPELS'

This may seem a trivial theme to include, however it was partly an enquiry by a highly educated Muslim research scholar which led to my writing this book. The knowledgeable Christian friend and I, to whom the question was addressed, were both unaware of the importance attached by some Muslims to stories told in the Koran (but not the Bible!) of Jesus' early life. We had to find out for ourselves. At the end of 3.6., we found the Koran telling us that the Baby Jesus spoke. We may be surprised to learn from this and other Koran passages that Muslims appear to know more of the early life of Jesus Christ than the average Christian. Mary's name occurs more often in the Koran than in the New Testament. How can this be? The Gospel writers had all met Mary, and Luke, the physician, may have spoken to her most about Jesus' birth, though Luke's information was certainly confirmed directly by the Holy Spirit.

A number of so-called 'Infancy Gospels', forming part of what is sometimes called the New Testament Apocrypha, were written to satisfy the hunger and curiosity for stories of the life of Jesus, and indeed of Mary, in what the true Gospel writers rightly leave as the 'silent years'. These were written long before Muhammad learned of them; he simply incorporated some of them in the Koran. All sorts of miracles performed by the infant Jesus, some fanciful and lurid, were concocted, covering in particular His early babyhood at Bethlehem and the flight to Egypt, but extending into His later childhood. Surah 3:46 reads "*He will speak to the people in the cradle and in maturity.*" After the half-heartedly accepted dictate of Constantine that his empire was officially Christian, these no doubt helped to compensate for the now debunked tales of old Greek mythology, which had been popular in that they had made few if any truly spiritual demands. In fact Jesus performed no miracles until His baptism and formal identification as the Lamb of God by His forerunner, John (Jn 1:29,36), although Satan had previously tempted Him to perform two miracles (Lk 4:3,9). The implications of prior claimed miracles are in fact dangerous, but too profound to discuss here.

It is worth stressing to Muslims that, of our four Gospels, only two relate the nativity happenings. Matthew takes Jesus' human ancestry back to Abraham, whom, as we shall see in Chapter 4, most Arabs count, along with Jews, as a common ancestor, whilst Luke takes this ancestry back to Adam, confirming His

The Theology of Islam

kinship with all men and women. However Mark omits such matters altogether and starts with the baptising for repentance ministry of Christ's Forerunner, John the Baptist immediately before the outset of the Messianic Mission, while the remaining Gospel, John, starts with a clear declaration of the Divinity and pre-existence of Christ (Jn 1:2-3,14,34), rather than elaborating on His human advent.

Regarding Jesus' birth and early life, in contrast with the Koran, the Gospels tell us only of His 'Nativity' (from the announcement of His miraculous conception, through His birth to His circumcision in compliance with the Law) and of His coming-of-age, when He went with His parents to Jerusalem. The flight to and return from Egypt are recorded in the Bible, but are not described in detail. That is what God the Holy Spirit in inspiring Holy Scripture chose to reveal to us, and we should be content with this, rather than devising (or believing) obscure, baseless stories to satisfy the curiosity of those who should be concentrating on the great truths of Christ's Person and purpose in coming into the world as Man.

As already remarked, the Koran acknowledges, and many Muslims are aware of this, the miraculous conception and birth of Jesus, even if the true nature of that miracle is not understood. The Koran's strange version of the 'Nativity' is found in Surah 19:1-36. From v 7 Zechariah (Zacharias) is told by an angel that he will have a son to be called John, not a traditional family name. Zechariah enquires how this can be, considering his *"extreme great age"*, but is told that this is easy with Allah. Zechariah, as he is about to emerge from the *"prayer chamber"* (compare the Bible's Temple) asks for a sign and is told that he will be dumb for three days – much briefer than in the Bible original!

At Surah 19:16 the narrative moves to Mary: *"And mention, [O Muhammad] in the Book [the story of] Mary, when she withdrew from her family to a place towards the east. And she took, in seclusion from them, a screen. Then we sent to her*

Our angel [i.e. Gabriel], and he represented himself to her as a well proportioned man. She said, 'Indeed I seek refuge in the Most Merciful from you, [so leave me], if you should be fearing of Allah.'" Not surprisingly there is some debate among Muslim scholars as to Gabriel's supposed role! R W Maqsood states that Gabriel is sometimes thought of by Muslims as the Holy Spirit. Referring again to Gabriel, the text continues in v 19: *'"He said, 'I am only the messenger of your Lord to give you [news of] a pure boy [i.e. a son].' She said 'How can I have while no man has touched me, and I have not been unchaste?'"* That statement at least could have been taken straight from the New Testament. Then it is said that this is easy, without offering a simple explanation of the means, as in Lk 1:35. Then the Koran text moves to an astonishing confusion with the birth of Ishmael in Gen 31:14-19, where Mary is said to have gone to a remote place and given birth under a palm tree where dates are miraculously provided for her and where her Son is said to have been born, only thereafter presenting Him to her family members, who admit that this event is without precedent (Surah 19:26-27). Then – wait for it - she, Mary (or Miryam in most versions) is addressed as Aaron's sister!!! And it is the Baby who is said to answer: *"[Jesus] said. 'Indeed I am the servant of Allah'"* (v 30).

Only when our Lord reached the priestly age of thirty, when He was baptised by John, tempted by the Devil and made His "Mission Statement" for His First Coming (Lk 4:16-21), are we told of His further words, deeds, ministry, rejection, trial, death, resurrection and ascension. Regarding these latter key events, we find direct denials and distortions in Islam.

3.9. ISLAMIC DENIAL OF CHRIST'S DEATH
Muslims say that Jesus could not have died, because Allah would not have allowed an innocent man to die for the sins of others; there is of course an inescapable human logic there. Whether Allah would have allowed it, however, is not the question, whether God did is what matters, and everything in the New Testament confirms that He most certainly died, and

the Old Testament foretold His death too: *"But he was wounded for our transgressions, he was bruised for our iniquities: the chastisement of our peace was upon him; and with his stripes we are healed. All we like sheep have gone astray; we have turned every one to his own way; and the LORD hath laid on him the iniquity of us all"* (Isa 53:5-6). The Koran can offer nothing on this Divine scale. Paul wrote: *"But **we preach Christ crucified**, unto Jews a stumblingblock, and unto Gentiles foolishness; but unto them that are called, both Jews and Greeks, Christ the power of God, and the wisdom of God"* (I Cor 1:23-24 ASV). What further proof do we need that Muhammad knew nothing of the power or wisdom of God?

What all four Gospels emphatically teach in the plainest possible terms, though each with certain different details and emphases, is that Jesus, in compliance with prophecy, really died as the result of His crucifixion, and on the third day rose literally out from among the dead. *"Him, being delivered by the determinate counsel and foreknowledge of God, ye have taken, and by wicked hands have crucified and slain: Whom God hath raised up, having loosed the pains of death: because it was not possible that he should be holden of it"* (Acts 2:23-24). The Divine counsel and foreknowledge of God is cast iron proof that this was central to His purposes, and was neither an accident nor an afterthought, but is beyond human, and especially Islamic, understanding.

Muslims require to be told politely but firmly that anything which purports to be Christianity and denies these truths is not Christianity. The Koran's presentation of Jesus Christ, even although it may be perceived as positive, is completely invalid. It teaches, and other Islamic writings support this supposition, that Jesus did not actually die; He merely appeared to die and was taken to Heaven by Allah. As we shall see at 7.2., this assumption is essential to Islamic end-time prophecy, where *'Jesus the Son of Miriam'* is to return to earth in the future and then die! **Now, without Jesus Christ having already died and risen again already, there can be no Christian Gospel, no salvation, no**

resurrection of the believing dead. No compromise is possible. Biblical proofs abound. Consider these texts: *"If Christ be not raised, your faith is vain; ye are yet in your sins"* (I Cor 15:17). No wonder Christians are prepared to be martyred for their faith! One need hardly point out that none can be raised from the dead without having died first! *"But now is Christ risen from the dead, and become the firstfruits of them that slept"* (1 Cor 15:20). *"Christ being raised from the dead dieth no more; death hath no more dominion over him"* (Rom 6:9).

Any nominal Christians who deny Christ's death are actually commended within the Koran, and those who believe in it are cursed by Allah and his followers. What an incredible lie it is to teach that God and Allah are one and the same when we read this. Moreover Christ's death is portrayed in the Koran as an affront to Mary: *"Allah has cursed them for their disbelief, so they believe not except for a few. And [We cursed them] for their disbelief and their saying against Mary a great slander. And [for] their saying: 'Indeed we have killed the Messiah, Jesus the son of Mary, the messenger of Allah.' And they did not kill him, nor did they crucify him, but [another] was made to resemble him to them. And indeed those who differ over it are in doubt about it. They have no knowledge of it except the following of assumption."* (Surah 4:155-157). Islam teaches, in other words, that Jesus' crucifixion was a confidence trick – an assertion worthy of the Father of Lies. How will they answer Jesus Christ when they have to stand before Him at His Great White Throne?

If Christ has not died, He cannot have been raised from the dead, and the spiritual condition of the believer is a hopeless one. I quote briefly from section 2.2.of my book, *"Rapture Sooner Not Later",* where references are NKJV:-

"Without Jesus' bodily resurrection, there is no Christianity, no hope, no assurance, no salvation: *"If you confess with your mouth the Lord Jesus and believe in your heart that **God has raised Him from the dead,** you will be saved'*

(Rom 10:9) *'If there is no resurrection of the dead, then Christ is not risen. And if Christ is not risen, then our preaching is empty and your faith is also empty.... For if the dead do not rise, then Christ is not risen. And **if Christ is not risen,** your faith is futile; **you are still in your sins!**'* (I Cor 15:13-15,17)..... But virtually all Bible-believing Christians, irrespective of tradition or denomination, do believe, and there is therefore no need in this book to argue that case. This is a work of the Holy Spirit: *'But if the Spirit of Him who raised Jesus from the dead dwells in you, He who raised Christ from the dead will also give life to your mortal bodies through His Spirit who dwells in you'* (Rom 8:11). The Holy Spirit bears witness: *'But we also who have the firstfruits of the Spirit, even we ourselves groan within ourselves, eagerly waiting for the adoption, the redemption of our body'* (Rom 8:23). Our salvation is sealed from the moment of our conversion, and was indeed foreknown by God from eternity. But the whole process is complete only when *this mortal puts on immortality.* Our bodily resurrection is no add-on afterthought or supplementary benefit."

Obviously we could add a great deal more from Holy Scripture.

3.10. SALVATION AND THE PILLARS OF ISLAM

We must soon leave this study of comparative theology. But before doing so we must note the infinitely wide gulf between the Christian means of salvation and the Islamic; and yet in the Koran one frequently sees glimpses of Muhammad's misunderstanding and adaptation of Christian soteriology (the doctrine of salvation). Surah16:61 reads: *"And if Allah were to impose blame on the people for their wrongdoing, He would not have left upon it [i.e. the earth] any creature."* This certainly implies mercy, but without the costly provision of restitution on Allah's part. To the human mind, this is plausible and acceptable.

Islam is a religion of ritual, works and submission. Christianity is not; but sadly for almost two thousand years many churches have been striving to make it so. Paul, writing to the Galatians, endeavoured vigorously to reverse the trend. Islam and apostate Christianity have had very different builders; but one can often detect the style of the same architect.

We saw back at 1.5. something of the difference between being 'born again' in the two faiths. Paul rightly said: *"For by grace are ye saved through faith; and that not of yourselves: it is the gift of God: Not of works, lest any man should boast"* (Eph 2:8-9) and: *"By the deeds of the law there shall no flesh be justified in his (God's) sight: for by the law is the knowledge of sin"* (Rom 3:20). Muslims, in contrast, concentrate on practice rather than belief, for there can be no salvation within Islam except by works, even if such fast-track works as martyrdom are claimed to provide short-cuts to Heaven, irrespective of the catastrophic consequences for innocent victims. Their Imams and other religious leaders increasingly tell their young people that martyrdom will guarantee a place in Paradise. One cannot but wonder why these same leaders do not choose the same route; is this a cynical confidence trick to urge their devotees into doing something they would be afraid to do themselves? There is within Islam no possibility of personal assurance such as Christians can experience in Christ.

However we must admit that there are millions upon millions who call themselves Christians, as well as Christian derived cults, who, deceived by one of Satan's most dastardly lies, hope to gain eternal life through works. No doubt enquiring Muslims will have encountered these, and they can hardly be blamed for not discerning between the true Gospel and the wisdom of the world as applied to Christianity. Human nature sees eternal destinies being decided by the balance of good and evil deeds. Our God deals with sin for ever on a just and legal basis: *"For he hath made him (Jesus Christ) to be sin for us, who knew no sin; that we might be made the righteousness of God in him"* (II Cor 5:21). Any forgiveness on Allah's part is thought of as being arbitrary.

The Theology of Islam

Central to works, which are thought to gain spiritual merit for Muslims. are the Five Pillars of Islam. Whether they practise them or not, most Muslims take these seriously. They are derived from the Koran, rather than taken directly from it, and differ somewhat from region to region within Islam. The following is the briefest of summaries of a common list, derived from the immensely helpful: *"Pocket Guide to Islam"* (FFM 1992), with added comments from a variety of sources.

- *Tashahhad* or confessing the faith. Some Muslims extend this to **holy war or Jihad to which any male Muslim can be legally summoned**.
- *Salat* or prayer. This is ritualistic and repetitive, with the forehead touching the ground, and must be done five times a day, facing Mecca, by older children and adults except those seriously physically impaired or incapacitated. Requirements vary locally and have been sometimes modified or adapted to circumstances, although there are always fanatical leaders who demand the most rigorous observance. Visit the average mosque and you will notice the meagre amount of space allocated to women for prayer, compared with men; spiritually, in this life and the next, women tend to be regarded as second class citizens.
- *Saum* or fasting. This applies particularly to daylight hours during the ninth lunar month of *Ramadan.* The minute details of this observance, which can, for instance, include tiny details as toothpaste, are reminiscent of the hypocritical tithing by the Pharisees, which Jesus censured, of mint, anise and cumin (Matt 13:13)
- *Zakat* or alms giving. The rules for giving alms to the poor are intricate and vary somewhat geographically. Many Muslims give only to other Muslims, but much publicity has recently been given to charitable donations, some generous, to the needy of other faiths. This must be acknowledged.
- *Hajj* or pilgrimage to Mecca. This involves completing

85

a variety of rituals, such as shaving the head and kissing the black stone of the Ka'abah. At one time this was considered obligatory only to males living within reasonable travelling distance of Mecca. Those whose pilgrimages had been from afar were, in some cultures, able to prefix *Hadji* (spellings varied) to their surnames. With modern transport facilities the *Hajj* has come within reach of millions upon millions of Muslims.

Before leaving the key theme of salvation, let us return briefly to the Islamic phenomenon of Kismet, mentioned briefly in the final bullet point of section 3.3. Kismet is a form of fatalism, it is unique to Islam. Yet surprisingly it has a counterpart within conservative Christianity, even in what claims to be evangelical Christianity! It is the equally fatalistic phenomenon of Calvinism or 'Reformed' theology, which teaches that God foreordained who would go to Heaven and who to Hell, without the individual having any choice in the matter, contrary to the assurance, *"For whom he did **foreknow**, he also did predestinate to be conformed to the image of his Son"* (Rom 8:29). Its reverse logic fails to see that God's predestination is based upon His Divine foreknowledge and not vice versa. It ignores such wonderful truths as: *"The Lord..... is **not willing that any should perish**, but that all should come to repentance"* (II Pet 3:9); *"God our Saviour; Who will have **all men to be saved**, and to come unto the knowledge of the truth"* (I Tim 2:3-4). All men certainly will not be saved, far from it, but that is not God's will. It applies human logic to certain texts taken out of context, forgetting that *"the preaching of the cross is to them that perish foolishness; but unto us which are saved it is the power of God"* (I Cor 1:18,) or that *"For after that in the wisdom of God the world by wisdom knew not God, it pleased God by the foolishness of preaching to save them that believe"* (I Cor 1:21). Rather, they embrace one of the greatest possible disincentives to preaching the Cross, assuming that some are going to be saved and others lost anyway. They forget that He who said: *"Ye have not chosen me, but I have chosen you"* (Jn 15:16) is the One who also said: *"Let him that is athirst come.*

The Theology of Islam

And **whosoever will**, let him take the water of life freely" (Rev 22:17). CH Spurgeon admitted that he could not understand this apparent enigma, but he knew beyond any shadow of doubt that the Bible taught it, and preached accordingly, winning many thousands for Christ. Happily, because many of those, including some leaders, whose denominations officially teach this so called Reformed Theology are actually born again believers, the indwelling Holy Spirit overrules the falsehood, and their natural reaction as children of God is "*Woe is unto me, if I preach not the gospel!*" (I Cor 9:16). John de Silva's inexpensive little book *"Calvinism – Bitter For Sweet"* (see Bibliography) is a wonderfully succinct exposure of this growing threat.

3.11. BEATITUDES WHICH ISLAM CANNOT EQUAL

Before we leave the topics of Islamic theology, rituals and duties, let us take note of how eloquently the Beatitudes, recorded in Matt 5:1-12, provide evidence that Islam has no claim to a Biblical heritage. Muhammad **went up into a mountain** and encountered some being masquerading as Gabriel and was given the Koran; contrast that with the following: *"And seeing the multitudes, he (Jesus) went up into a mountain: and when he was set, his disciples came unto him: And he opened his mouth, and taught them, saying, Blessed are the poor in spirit: for theirs is the kingdom of heaven. Blessed are they that mourn: for they shall be comforted. Blessed are the meek: for they shall inherit the earth. Blessed are they which do hunger and thirst after righteousness: for they shall be filled. Blessed are the merciful: for they shall obtain mercy. Blessed are the pure in heart: for they shall see God. Blessed are the peacemakers: for they shall be called the children of God. Blessed are they which are persecuted for righteousness' sake: for theirs is the kingdom of heaven."* Try comparing these gracious words with the Koran. There is no comparison. On the one hand we have the peerless declarations of the Son of God; on the other we have the hate-ridden diatribes of one who fumed because Christians would not accept him as being superior to Jesus Christ. The Beatitudes, of course, do not constitute a recipe for salvation, which is just as well, for few of us measure up to all of these standards; but we should do.

The final Beatitude puts the martyrdom of so many Christians at the hands of Muslims into the perspective of eternity: "*Blessed are ye, when men shall revile you, and persecute you, and shall say all manner of evil against you falsely, for my sake. Rejoice, and be exceeding glad: for great is your reward in heaven: for so persecuted they the prophets which were before you.*"

We are now in a position to look briefly at the claimed pre-history of Islam and the Bible revealed history of God's dealing with Israel from the time of Abraham, the common ancestor of Israelite and Arab. We will see how faithfully predictive prophecy has been fulfilled in the past, as a guarantee of how unfulfilled prophecies will be fulfilled in the future.

CHAPTER FOUR

The Antecedents of Two Faiths

And God said unto Abraham...."In Isaac shall thy seed be called. And also of the son of the bondwoman will I make a nation, because he is thy seed".
(Gen 21:12-13)

4.1. WHY BOTHER?

This chapter is important, because it is to Abraham that God promised His greatest blessing of all - One Who was to be both Abraham's Son according to the flesh and the Son of God, the means of salvation to all who would receive Him in an eternally valid legal and righteous transaction, rather than merely as a gesture of goodwill on God's part. It is essential that we should understand how this blessing to Abraham was to be executed and why the Holy Spirit has devoted so many chapters of Genesis to the early selection of the Messianic human blood-line. And, as we shall see, God, in His greater wisdom broke with human tradition in choosing two younger sons, rather than their firstborn brethren. The response of the offspring of the disqualified elder sons has been one of bitterness, resentment, jealousy, hatred and enmity, which has lasted 4,000 years, and is set, as we shall see in Chapters 6 and 7, to extend to the end of this age.

Except when quoting Scripture, I shall use the New Testament practice of referring to the Patriarch and his wife by their covenant names, 'Abraham' and 'Sarah', although from Genesis 11 until 17 they actually appear as Abram, meaning 'father of heights' and Sarai, meaning 'Jah is Prince'. God renamed them Abraham, 'father of a multitude' and Sarah, 'princess'.

Every descendant of Abraham outside that God ordained bloodline has been at enmity with Israel every time she has existed as a recognisable national entity. And, let us make no mistake, however much we may love her for the Lord's sake, Israel herself has frequently abused her privileged position, even rejecting the Messiah Whom she had brought forth. In consequence she has throughout the Church Age been side-lined in God's purposes. And now, as she gradually comes back 'on track' in those purposes, she is caught between the antipathy of her ancient rivals and rejection by the majority of the largely Gentile Christian church, hitherto the main beneficiaries of Abraham's blessing.

So in this chapter we will examine why the enmity between Jew and Arab is more than 4,000 years old, and why the rivalry between Christianity and Islam has roots long before the 7th Century. In the perspective of time and eternity it goes back to the Book of Genesis, and in particular to events recorded from chapters twelve to thirty-six. Judaism and Christianity recognise the younger son of Abraham, Isaac, the child of promise, and Muslims recognise Ishmael, the elder son of Abraham, the child of impatience and compromise.

Muslims are sensitive about Israel and such limited support Israel has had over the past century from Christian nations. They are more likely to be impressed by arguments from the Bible, a book held with considerable reverence by Muslims since the time of the Prophet himself, though naturally never accorded the infallible status which the Koran has since enjoyed. Take them back to both the **conditional and unconditional** prophecies concerning Israel, and be careful to distinguish between these.

4.2. FROM ADAM TO ABRAHAM

Many years ago a missionary society translated the New Testament into the local language and seemed to make little progress. When they later translated Genesis, the reaction was "*Now* we understand!" The greatest religious schism of all occurred between the Gospel of Grace, as foreshadowed by

The Antecedents of Two Faiths

Abel's Lamb, and the Gospel of Works, as represented by Cain and his rejected bodily efforts to atone for the sin of his soul. Abel's faith was carried forward within Seth's line,

Many basic truths which are not recognised by other religions are more or less recognised by Islam and therefore do not have to be explained. Islam believes in angels and demons, which are called *jinns,* although not all are considered evil; these are the genies or genii found in the Arabian Nights and Aladdin. . These are often greatly feared. Satan or *Iblis* is seen as the chief *jinn*. They believe in Heaven and Hell, about both of which we will have more to say in Chapter 6. Rather than seeing the Fall having taken place in an earthly Garden of Eden, they believe that Adam's and Eve's plunge was from Heaven to earth - compare Satan's falls past and future (Isa 14:12, Lk 10:18, Rev 12:9). Muhammad's assumption that the future restored earthly environment in the Bible is Paradise is illustrated in Surah 7.19: *"And, 'O Adam, dwell, you and your wife, in Paradise and eat from wherever you will, but do not approach this tree, lest you be among the wrongdoers.'"*

At least Satan is blamed for Adam's and Eve's downfall - but from Heaven, rather than within the newly created earth. Adam, who is never called a prophet in the Bible, is still revered by Muslims as a prophet and the original builder of the Ka'abah, a shrine erected in gratitude for God's forgiveness – interesting when one considers that, such were Adam's and Eve's lack of manual skills, that God had to prepare skins to cover their nakedness (Gen 3:21), and especially when one learns that the Ka'abah is fifteen metres in height and built of stone blocks; perhaps those were not considered to be the original dimensions. Because it was supposed to be the first shrine of God on earth, it is still considered to have priority over any other places of worship including Jerusalem. Only Muslims are entitled to visit it; others are banned. This is all in contrast with Adam and Eve having been cast out of Eden **after** the promise of a Redeemer from their seed. (Gen 3:15). Noah, not all of whose sons are said by

Islam to have been prepared to enter the Ark and be saved from the Flood, is also revered as a prophet.

Much of what we know of antediluvian religion is through what, having evidently been preserved in the mind of Ham within the Ark, was developed by his grandson, Nimrod. The legacy of this antediluvian religion is summarised in these verses: *"And GOD saw that the wickedness of man was great in the earth, and that every imagination of the thoughts of his heart was only evil continually..... The earth also was corrupt before God, and the earth was filled with violence"* (Gen 6:5,11). After the Flood *"God blessed Noah and his sons, and said unto them, Be fruitful, and multiply, and **replenish the earth**"* (Gen 9:1). But on the plain of Shinar, later the site of Babylon, they defied God's instruction: *"And they said, Go to, let us build us a city and a tower, whose top may reach unto heaven; and let us make us a name, **lest we be scattered** abroad upon the face of the whole earth"* (Gen 11:4). God therefore forcibly scattered them, probably speeding up continental drift in the still pliable earth's surface to accelerate the process (see Gen 11:25).

Religious diversification followed, but some ancient demi-gods, such as the Mother (Semiramis) and the miraculously conceived Child and pseudo-saviour (Tammuz), were widely retained, reappearing among the dispersed nations as, for instance, the Isis and Osiris in Egypt, the Isi and Iswara in India, and other well-known names in the mythology of ancient Greece and Rome, Hinduism, Buddhism and Taoism, not to mention the Roman Catholic Church. Their remarkably similar Madonna and Child images are widespread in temples and chapels – I saw two in temples on the island of Labuan off the Borneo coast, which looked remarkably similar to one in a grotto in Lanarkshire! But God called Abraham away from all this idolatry, although his kinsman Laban still retained those household idols with which Rachel absconded (Gen 31:19), and even Jacob had to warn his family against them (35:1). Muhammad is to be commended for having rejected all these, as we saw in Chapter 2, when he embraced the monotheism of Abraham (or Ibrahim in the Koran), although one cannot help but notice the frequency in the Koran, compared with the Bible, of the **joint** mentions of Mary and Jesus, as we saw at 3.7.

4.3. THE PATRIARCH CONNECTION

As remarked earlier, while the Gentile orientated Gospel of Luke takes Jesus' human ancestry back to Adam, the Jewish Messianic emphasised Gospel of Matthew takes us back only as far as Abraham, the point at which ethnically the Jews and first Arabs emerge. The Quraish (or Quarysh) tribe of Muhammad claimed to be descended directly from Abraham's first son, Ishmael, whose mother was Hagar, bondservant of Abraham's wife, Sarah. There is no need to question this claim of descent; Unger's Bible Dictionary points out that, although names are lost before the twenty-first generation before the Prophet, the pre-Mohammedan law of blood revenge required a detailed knowledge of at least four generations. Thus genealogies were strictly and jealously maintained in the Middle East in those days, and we know that once the Children of Israel were settled in the Promised Land, Isaac's descendants from Esau became nations which formed an eastern and south-eastern buffer screen between them and the Ishmaelite settlements.

Although both in Judaism and Islam Abraham is considered the first Patriarch, Genesis 11:27 takes us back a generation to Terah, the father of Abram, Nahor and Haran, the extended family within which early marriages, such as those of Isaac and Jacob, were permitted. These were the progenitors of a number of Semitic nations which feature in Old Testament prophecy and history, and who are considered by God to be relations of the Jewish people. The Philistines and Canaanites, members of the nations which God ordered Israel under Joshua to dispossess, were all descendants of Noah's son, Ham, and are therefore not Semitic. Ishmael and Esau are recorded in Genesis as having married women outside Terah's family, thus tainting at the outset their Semitic ancestry.

4.4. RIVALRY OF ISHMAEL'S AND ISAAC'S MOTHERS

The history of the Patriarchs is long and complex, occupying all except the first eleven chapters of Genesis. We will have to be selective. The rift between the two mothers may initially have seemed trivial, but ultimately it led to diametrically opposite (in substance) faiths and, as we shall see, to a theme picked up in the New Testament epistles. It was all part of the narrowing and channelling of the Messianic line from Noah to the Saviour's birth.

Long before Abraham had any children, God made a promise to him; the book of Genesis dates to Moses' time and uses the Name Yahweh or Jehovah, but none of the ancients ever addressed Him thus: *"Now Jehovah said unto Abram, Get thee out of thy country, and from thy kindred, and from thy father's house, unto the land that I will show thee: and I will make of thee a great nation, and I will bless thee, and make thy name great; and be thou a blessing; and I will bless them that bless thee, and him that curseth thee will I curse: and in thee shall all the families of the earth be blessed"* (Gen 12:1-3 ASV). Abraham was a man of great faith: *"And he believed in Jehovah; and he reckoned it to him for righteousness"* (Gen 15:6 ASV); he was specially commended for this faith in Heb 11:8-9. He had faith in both God's temporal and eternal promises: *"By faith he sojourned in the land of promise, as in a strange country, dwelling in tabernacles with Isaac and Jacob, the heirs with him of the same promise: For he looked for a city which hath foundations, whose builder and maker is God"* (Heb 11:9-10). Tabernacles here are tents. A multitude of other prophecies confirm that **the eternal promises did not negate the temporal ones**, as some theologians wrongly assume. The Bible account of Abraham's life negates Islamic claims that he and Ishmael rebuilt the Ka'abah; Abraham's various journeys are all listed in the Bible, and the very long expedition to Mecca and back would surely have been related – had it taken place.

But even Abraham faltered once as he approach old age and

The Antecedents of Two Faiths

infertility, and so acted on Sarah's suggestion to have a child by Hagar (Hajaraha in the Koran), to allow this promise to be fulfilled. It was almost as if Abraham and Sarah were offering God a way out of a perceived problem which was to God no problem! But in fact God intended to stretch their faith to the point where the necessary offspring was to be a miraculous answer to prayer. *"Through faith also Sara herself received strength to conceive seed, and was delivered of a child when she was past age, because she judged him faithful who had promised. Therefore sprang there even of one, and him **as good as dead**, so many as the stars of the sky in multitude, and as the sand which is by the sea shore innumerable"* (Heb 11:11-12). But earlier Hagar had conceived and openly despised her mistress, Sarah (Gen 16:4). She fled from Sarah's anger, and the Angel of the Lord, who was almost certainly the pre-incarnate Christ Himself, appeared to her: *"And the angel of the LORD said unto her, I will multiply thy seed exceedingly, that it shall not be numbered for multitude. And the angel of the LORD said unto her, Behold, thou art with child, and shalt bear a son, and shalt call his name Ishmael; because the LORD hath heard thy affliction. And he will be a wild man; his hand will be against every man, and every man's hand against him; and he shall dwell in the presence of all his brethren"* (Gen 16:10-12). The word *'presence'* in the AV should be *'face'*, indicating constant quarrelsome facing up to. How very accurate and descriptive that last prophecy is of both the ancestors and members of Islam.

Later God enlarged His original covenant with Abraham: *"As for me, behold, my covenant is with thee, and thou shalt be a father of many nations. Neither shall thy name any more be called Abram, but thy name shall be Abraham; for a father of many nations have I made thee. And I will make thee exceeding fruitful, and I will make nations of thee, and kings shall come out of thee. And I will establish my covenant between me and thee and thy seed after thee in their generations for an everlasting covenant, to be a God unto thee, and to thy seed after thee. And I will give unto thee, and to thy seed after thee, the land wherein thou art a stranger, all the land of Canaan, for an everlasting possession; and I will be their God"* (Gen 17:4-8). It was now not simply *"a great nation"*, as it might have been but for Ishmael, but *"many nations"*. This title to the Land has never been revoked, but occupation has always been conditional – more in Chapter 5.

Abraham, as a very natural father, was conscious both of the Sarah-Hagar animosity and his own lack of any other offspring: *"And Abraham said unto God, O that Ishmael might live before thee! And God said, Sarah thy wife shall bear thee a son indeed; and thou shalt call his name Isaac: and I will establish my covenant with him for an everlasting covenant, and with his seed after him. And as for Ishmael, I have heard thee: Behold, I have blessed him, and will make him fruitful, and will multiply him exceedingly; twelve princes shall he beget, and I will make him a great nation.* **But my covenant will I establish with Isaac**, *which Sarah shall bear unto thee at this set time in the next year"* (Gen 17:18-21). The angelic deputation and assurance of Sarah's forthcoming motherhood is related in Gen 18:1-15: *"Now Abraham and Sarah were old and well stricken in age; and it ceased to be with Sarah after the manner of women"* (18:11).

Note the potential for conflict between the Ishmaelite tribes or nations, which had been promised by God, and the twelve tribes of the Children of Jacob or Israel, son of the promised Isaac. God's unconditional prophecies never fail, even if the pace and timescales are not necessarily what we expect them to be. God not only allowed Sarah the ability to conceive and give birth to this child, but apparently completely restored her youth in the process, because in Genesis 20 we find that the Philistine king, Ahimelech, found Sarah attractive and would have married her had she been free to do so. Abraham was likewise restored and, apparently after Sarah's death, although the Hebrew is not absolutely clear here, when he was 137 years old married again and had six sons by Keturah. But none of this altered Isaac's status as heir to the promise; *"And Abraham gave all that he had unto Isaac. But unto the sons of the concubines, which Abraham had, Abraham gave gifts, and sent them away from Isaac his son, while he yet lived, eastward, unto the east country"* (Gen 25:5-6). In time their identity became merged with the Ishmaelites.

Most of Abraham's children by Hagar and Keturah and their descendants, settled to the east, the future cradle of Islam, Abraham was indeed the father of nations other than Israel. As Muhammad and his tribe made no claim to be descended from Isaac, we can keep any remarks on Esau and Isaac brief.

People have criticised the behaviour of Sarah towards Hagar, and yet God vindicated her: *"And Sarah saw the son of Hagar the Egyptian, which she had born unto Abraham, mocking. Wherefore she said unto Abraham, Cast out this bondwoman and her son: for the son of this bondwoman shall not be heir with my son, even with Isaac. And the thing was very grievous in Abraham's sight because of his son. And **God said** unto Abraham, Let it not be grievous in thy sight because of the lad, and because of thy bondwoman; in all that Sarah hath said unto thee, hearken unto her voice; for in Isaac shall thy seed be called. And also of the son of the bondwoman will I make a nation, because he is thy seed"* (Gen 21:9-13). Hagar had not heeded her first lesson and suffered the consequences. Paul, in Gal 4:21 to 31 confirms the historicity of these events, if we really need proof, and uses the bondwoman and freewoman as an allegory; please note the fuller remarks at 4.9.

4.5. CONTRASTING VERSIONS OF ABRAHAM'S GREATEST TEST

The Bible says, *"Cast out the Bondwoman and her son."* In effect the Koran says, "Cast out the freewoman and her son and reinstate the bondwoman and her son. This is vividly illustrated in the Islamic version of Abraham's sacrifice in Genesis 22, written around 2,700 years after the event. Actually the account is very brief in the Koran and has been supplemented by the Hadith traditions to become a charming tale, but with the key element removed. The Koran does not actually name Ishmael, but, as in the Koran Isaac is demonstrated not to have been born at the time, the strongly held ancient Islamic tradition that it was Ishmael confirms this view. More than five and a half centuries before the Koran, the writer to the Hebrews records: *"By faith Abraham, when he was tried, offered up Isaac: and he that had received the promises offered up his only begotten son, Of whom it was said, That in Isaac shall thy seed be called: Accounting that God was able to raise him up, even from the dead; from whence also he received him in a figure"* (Heb 11:17-19).

In the Bible this event was a key link in the great doctrine of the Lamb, which commenced with Abel and can be traced through Old and New Testaments to Revelation 22, a doctrine evidently abhorrent to the spiritual sponsor of the Koran. I devote a little space here, because the following can be explained thoughtfully to a Muslim, hopefully without causing too much offence.

- In Genesis 4:3-12 the need and acceptability of the Lamb is emphasised.
- In the Genesis 22 passage which we are reviewing it is God's rather than mankind's provision of the Lamb which is in view. It is here that the truth of *Jehovah Jireh* is revealed – the *"God Who provides"*, a central element in the Gospel of Grace, *"That in the ages to come he might shew the exceeding riches of his grace in his kindness toward us through Christ Jesus. For by grace are ye saved through faith; and that not of yourselves: **it is the gift of God: Not of works**, lest any man should boast"* (Eph 2:7-9).
- In the Passover, as ordained in Exodus chapter 12, it is the death of the Lamb and efficacy of the blood which are especially explained: *"And the blood shall be to you for a token upon the houses where ye are: and when I see the blood, I will pass over you, and the plague shall not be upon you to destroy you, when I smite the land of Egypt"* (12:13).
- In Levitical law two goats were chosen, as it would have

been inappropriate to have had two lambs for different purposes: *"And Aaron shall bring the goat upon which the LORD'S lot fell, and offer him for a sin offering. But the goat, on which the lot fell to be the scapegoat, shall be presented alive before the LORD, to make an atonement with him, and to let him go for a scapegoat into the wilderness"* (Lev 16:9-10). Both the vicarious death and the carrying away for ever of sin were thus represented.

- In Isaiah 53, the true Lamb is at last shown to be a Man rather than a mere animal, One who was to be judged for wayward human 'sheep': *"All we like sheep have gone astray; we have turned every one to his own way; and the LORD hath laid on him the iniquity of us all. He was oppressed, and he was afflicted, yet he opened not his mouth: he is brought as a lamb to the slaughter, and as a sheep before her shearers is dumb, so he openeth not his mouth"* (53:6-7).

- In John chapter 1, already quoted, that sin-bearing Man is shown to be Jesus: *"The next day John seeth Jesus coming unto him, and saith, Behold the Lamb of God, which taketh away the sin of the world."* (1:29).

- In Acts chapter 8, after Philip had expounded to him from the above quoted scroll of Isaiah, the Ethiopian eunuch confessed that Jesus, the Lamb of the passage he had just read, is the Christ, the Son of God. *"And Philip said, If thou believest with all thine heart, thou mayest. And he answered and said, I believe that Jesus Christ is the Son of God"* (Acts 8:37).

- Peter eloquently confirms that the death of the Lamb, Christ Jesus, was no afterthought or accident: *"Forasmuch as ye know that ye were not redeemed with corruptible things, as silver and gold..... But with the precious blood of Christ, as of a lamb without blemish and without spot: Who verily was foreordained before the foundation of the world"* (I Pet 1:18-20).

- In Revelation chapters 21 and 22 the risen and glorified

Lamb, the Son of God, is revealed as still being the Lamb during the Millennium which will follow His return in Power and even thereafter, giving all blood-bought believers eternal confidence that their names will not be excluded from the Lamb's Book of Life (21:27). The Lamb is mentioned seven times in the last two chapters of the Bible.

4.6. WHAT ACTUALLY HAPPENED ON THE MOUNTAIN

In the Bible the Genesis 22 event was a potent foreshadowing of Calvary, rather than a full 'pre-enactment', with God intervening at the crucial moment unlike at the Cross. The actual death of a human sacrifice could not be pre-empted. Isaac bore the wood, and his father the fire and the knife. The mount of sacrifice was Moriah, at Jerusalem, thought by Jews to be the Temple Mount and the very spot where the altar of sacrifice was in Solomon's Temple, rather than the nearby hill of Calvary or Golgotha. Isaac's question regarding the absence of a lamb for the burnt offering indicates that Abraham had not forewarned him; however he did not resist the binding.

Muslims readily admit that their version of Abraham's sacrifice was quite different, although they do at least recognise that this was a test of Abraham on God's part. For them it was Ishmael (Isma'il) whom Abraham was told in a dream that he was to sacrifice. Unlike the Bible version, he told the boy in advance what he was about to do, and he agreed to this, assuming that this was Allah's will. The Hadith elaborates by saying that Satan in disguise tried to dissuade Abraham from sacrificing his son, saying that only the Devil would ask him to do anything so wicked. Think of the subtle implications! Thereafter Satan unsuccessfully tried to tempt first Hagar and then Ishmael to resist. Then they all threw stones at Satan in disguise and drove him away! According to the Bible, Sarah and Hagar would have been three days' journey away.

Ishmael is said in the Koran to have been very keen that his father

The Antecedents of Two Faiths

should sacrifice him: *"He said. 'O my son, indeed I have seen in a dream that I [must] sacrifice you. To see what you think.' He said, 'O my father, do as you are commanded, you will find me, if Allah wills, of the steadfast.'"* (Surah 37:102). Even today in Islam martyrdom is a common aspiration. At the last moment, as in the Bible, Abraham was halted from slaying his son, having satisfied God as to his obedience. As in the Bible version, a ram was sacrificed instead; this is still being commemorated in the *Eid ul-Adha* sacrifice at the end of the *Hajj*.

In a very different ending in the Koran Abraham's faith was rewarded by the barren Sarah being given a son, Isaac – strange, in view of the fact that according to the much earlier Bible account, Isaac had already been around for several years!

4.7. ISAAC. ESAU AND JACOB

We should note that Abraham's inheritance through which *"all families of the earth be blessed"* (Gen 12:3) through the coming Christ and Saviour, is specifically passed on through Isaac and Jacob, both of whom had personal promises from God. To Isaac God said: *"And I will make thy seed to multiply as the stars of heaven, and will give unto thy seed all these countries; and in thy seed shall all the nations of the earth be blessed"* (Gen 26:4). To Jacob He said: *"I am God Almighty: be fruitful and multiply; a nation and a company of nations shall be of thee, and kings shall come out of thy loins; And the land which I gave Abraham and Isaac, to thee I will give it, and to thy seed after thee will I give the land"* (Gen 35:11-12.) God renamed Jacob, meaning 'supplanter', 'Israel', which means 'ruling with God', (Gen 35:10). Muslims and Replacement Theologians, please take careful note. So the chosen nation descended from Abraham through him became the Children of Israel, also Israelites and Hebrews and later Jews.

Isaac's wife, Rebekah, like her mother-in-law before her, has been criticised, in her case for her part in deceiving the almost blind Isaac into giving his blessing to the younger Jacob, rather than to the fractionally older Esau. But here it was Rebekah who perceived God's will rather than Isaac; she had been wise enough to seek to know that will at a time of crisis: *"And the children struggled together within her. And she said, If it be so, wherefore do I live? And she went to inquire of Jehovah. And Jehovah said unto her, Two nations are in thy womb, And two peoples shall be separated from thy bowels. And the one people shall be stronger than the other people. And the elder shall serve the younger"* (Gen 25:22-23 ASV). That struggle has never really ended, and for long the famous birthright has never been allowed to be forgotten. Rather it became a running sore, the cause of enmity throughout succeeding generations. Even today Antisemitism thrives on it.

Isaac was personally unhappy about having given his blessing to Jacob, rather than to Esau, the son whom he evidently preferred; but he was perceptive enough to realise that God had over-ruled and that he could not undo Jacob's blessing, though he was able to give a lesser blessing to Esau (see Heb 11:20): *"Then Isaac his father answered him: 'Behold, away from the fatness of the earth shall your dwelling be, and away from the dew of heaven on high.* **By your sword you shall live**, *and you shall serve your brother; but when you break loose you shall break his yoke from your neck'"* (Gen 27:39-40 RSV). The RSV is correct, compared to the AV etc, in stressing that he would live in arid desert regions. Need we comment about the sword? Muslims still confess that theirs is a religion of the sword.

4.8. PERCEPTIONS OF ISRAEL

The topic of Israel is like a red rag to a bull for most Muslims. However the subject simply cannot be avoided. It might be helpful to point out to them the common, though not universal, enmity between Christians and the Jews from the outset of the Church Age, initially from the Jewish side, but thereafter from the Christian side, with persecutions, expulsions, inquisitions, pogroms and holocausts, more recently in Russia and Germany, but earlier in England, Spain etc. It is also important to stress that even those Christians among us who love the Jews for the Lord's sake recognise that such suffering, persecution and isolation which the Jews have suffered down through the centuries has in effect been self-inflicted through disobedience, blindness and hardness of heart, but has been guaranteed by God Himself to have a future climactic ending, as we will be reminded in chapters 6 and 7.

It must be understood that being Jewish – or any other descendant of Abraham for that matter – is of no spiritual value when hearts are not right with God. It can be a greater liability than a blessing, because, as Jesus, in answering, said to the Pharisees, *"Ye shall know the truth, and the truth shall make you free. They answered him, We be Abraham's seed, and were never in bondage to any man: how sayest thou, Ye shall be made free?..... But now ye seek to kill me, a man that hath told you the truth, which I have heard of God: this did not Abraham"* (Jn 8:32-33,40). Jesus' answer was one of His most severe recorded: *"Ye are of your father the devil, and the lusts of your father ye will do. He was a murderer from the beginning, and abode not in the truth, because there is no truth in him"* (Jn 8:44). Human descent may impart privilege in this life, but is no ticket to Heaven. If some natural descendants are thus excluded, in Christ others may be included. As John Rice comments:

> "So, in a spiritual sense, Abraham is the father of all those who are saved."

He goes on to quote Gal 3:6-8: *"Even as Abraham believed God, and it was accounted to him for righteousness. Know ye therefore that they which are of faith, the same are the children of Abraham. And the scripture, foreseeing that God would justify the heathen through faith, preached before the gospel unto Abraham, saying, In thee shall all nations be blessed."* Now Dr Rice has a sound, balanced view. The danger arises when some assume that Jews are thereby for ever excluded and count for nothing in God's plans. In Chapter 6 and 7 we will see that this is emphatically not so. Hebrew Christians have a double descent from Abraham – physical and spiritual. In the next section we return to the Epistle to the Galatians, to see that the faith of Abraham foreshadows saving faith as expounded in the New Testament, rather than anything in the Koran.

Thus spiritually even Gentile believing Christians are descended from Abraham, and greatly outnumber his natural ones. In a similar way the majority of Muslims are not physically descended from Esau, or even from Ishmael. But in a sense they might be said to be spiritual descendants of Ishmael, and probably few would dispute that.

John Walvoord writes succinctly about a frustration experienced by teachers who give prophecy attention in inverse proportion to the space allocated to it in the Bible.

> "One of the main sources for current confusion in understanding prophecy is the failure to take Israel-related prophecy literally. Attempts to transfer the promises relating to Israel to the church have been a major obstacle to understanding God's prophetic purposes as a whole. Once prophecies about Israel are distinguished from prophecies concerning the church or the Gentiles, the main programs of God as outlined in prophecy begin to be clear."

Down through the centuries Christians, under the false assumption that they are the New Israel, assume that it is their responsibility to behave as a 'nation' in the way that Israel, with its unique covenant relationship with Jehovah, had. God's covenant relationship with Israel was unique and unrepeatable. Those who doubt this should consider the following facts about Israel:-

- A nation which God has for 4,000 years kept from integration: *"The people shall dwell alone, and shall not be reckoned among the nations"* (Numb 23:8-9).
- A nation blessed and Divinely preserved despite prolonged exiles: *"How shall I curse, whom God hath not cursed? or how shall I defy, whom the LORD hath not defied? "Surely there is no enchantment against*

The Antecedents of Two Faiths

Jacob, neither is there any divination against Israel" (Numb 23:8,23).
- The plagues upon Pharaoh and Egypt and crossing of the Red Sea.
- Manna provided and water miraculously drawn from the rock.
- The pillar of cloud by day and fire by night throughout their journeyings.
- Clothes and shoes that did not wear out for forty years (Deut 29:5).
- Overwhelming victories, sometimes against incredible odds.
- The explicit promises of guaranteed blessing and cursing in Deuteronomy 28 to 30 in a variety of situations, which no Christian or anybody else has been able to claim or apply, but which were often put to the test and verified, particularly in the book of Judges. Elsewhere God may indeed answer our requests for blessing or relief, but not with the same immediate guarantees: *"He maketh his sun to rise on the evil and on the good, and sendeth rain on the just and on the unjust"* (Matt 5:45).

We could continue this list for some time, but hopefully the above will prove the point, that these were unique dealings on God's part..

4.9. GALATIANS AND ISLAM

The little epistle of Galatians, which I have quoted only briefly, can be invaluable in countering the claims of Islam. Here is a consolidated list of examples which might form a basis for profitable discussion. They follow in a natural progressive sequence within the Epistle. Here I shall make the briefest comments, and shall be quoting the NKJV. This list is far from exhaustive:-
- *"But even if we, or an angel from heaven, preach any other gospel to you than what we have preached to you, let him be accursed"* (1:8). The Koran was

given to Muhammad by the angel Jibrel, claimed to be Gabriel.

- *"For I neither received it from man, nor was I taught it, but it came through the revelation of Jesus Christ"* (1:12). What higher authority can there be?
- *"I did not immediately confer with flesh and blood, nor did I go up to Jerusalem to those who were apostles before me; but I went to Arabia, and returned again to Damascus"* (1:16-17). Muhammad, being illiterate, immediately conferred with 'flesh and blood' to have his recitations recorded. Paul did not. Arabia has not been exclusive to Islam!
- *"Knowing that a man is not justified by the works of the law but by faith in Jesus Christ, even we have believed in Christ Jesus, that we might be justified by faith in Christ and not by the works of the law; for by the works of the law no flesh shall be justified"* (2:16). Christianity is a faith of grace, as with accepted Abel; Islam is a faith of works, as with rejected Cain.
- *"I have been crucified with Christ; it is no longer I who live, but Christ lives in me; and the life which I now live in the flesh I live by faith in the Son of God, who loved me and gave Himself for me"* (2:20). The Koran teaches that not only is Jesus Christ not the Son of God, but that He was not really crucified!
- *"Christ has redeemed us from the curse of the law, having become a curse for us (for it is written, 'Cursed is everyone who hangs on a tree'* (3:13). The Koran denies the vicarious nature of Christ's sacrifice. The Bible affirms it.
- *"That the blessing of Abraham might come upon the Gentiles in Christ Jesus, that we might receive the promise of the Spirit through faith"* (3:14). It is through Christ Jesus and not through Muhammad that Abraham's blessing comes.
- *Now to Abraham and his Seed were the promises made. He does not say, "And to seeds," as of many, but as of*

The Antecedents of Two Faiths

one, *"And to your Seed," who is Christ"* (3:16). In Luke's Gospel the "Seed of the woman" in God's promise to Eve, is traced to Abraham through Jacob and Isaac.

- *There is neither Jew nor Greek, there is neither slave nor free, there is neither male nor female; for you are all one in Christ Jesus. And if you are Christ's, then you are Abraham's seed, and heirs according to the promise"* (3:28-29). All three categories are still recognised by God, but not in the matter of our salvation, and we Gentile Christians can claim to be Abraham's seed. Islam cannot offer that.
- *For it is written that Abraham had two sons: the one by a bondwoman, the other by a freewoman......So then, brethren, we are not children of the bondwoman but of the free"* (Gal 4:22,31). This allegory, derived from actual history, is too long to quote in full. Christians are spiritual descendants of the freewoman and are not in bondage. *"Jerusalem which is now"* (v 25) is the unrepentant Jewish nation in the present dispensation – still in bondage and therefore spiritually children of Hagar, though physically of Isaac.
- *"For you, brethren, have been called to liberty; only do not use liberty as an opportunity for the flesh"* (5:13). In Christ we are given freedom, but never licence.
- *"Now the works of the flesh are evident, which are: adultery, fornication, uncleanness, lewdness, idolatry, sorcery, hatred, contentions, jealousies, outbursts of wrath, selfish ambitions, dissensions, heresies, envy, murders, drunkenness, revelries, and the like; of which I tell you beforehand, just as I also told you in time past, that those who practice such things will not inherit the kingdom of God"* (5:19-21). Contrast Christian freedom with the actions of the Jihadist.
- As we stressed back at 1.2., personal boasting is no way to approach Muslims. "*But God forbid that I should boast except in the cross of our Lord Jesus Christ, by whom the world has been crucified to me, and I to the world*

(6:14). When all our wonderful blessings come from God as a gift, we Christians have no right to boast. Were our blessing to result from the quality of our submission and observation of ritual, as hoped for by Muslims, we might possibly have such grounds!

4.10. DESCENDANTS OF LOT, ISHMAEL AND ESAU

During Israel's long sojourn in Egypt, the following blood tie nations were able to develop in their chosen territories.

- Ishmaelites Beginning at Gen 25:12 we have a detailed list of Ishmael's descendants. The eight volume Ellicott Commentary, which deals with these matters in depth, remarks: "Ishmael is not dismissed from the Divine presence without a short record of his history." Many of the names crop up in later books of the Old Testament, and Jetur as Iturea in Lk 3:1. However these three tribes or nations were neighbours, and thus buffer states between the Ishmaelites and Israel, which is why we see and hear less of Ishmael than of the others. The place names recorded in Genesis 25 show that the twelve Ishmaelite tribes came to dominate the Arabian Peninsula from Egypt to the Persian Gulf. Much of it now lies within Saudi Arabia.
- Ammon The Ammonites were incestuously descended from Lot by his younger daughter and her son, Ammon, so were descendants of Terah, Abraham's father, and therefore kinsfolk. The name is appropriately retained in Amman, the capital of modern Jordan. It lay on the eastern side of Jordan opposite the central tribes of Israel, and its people were pushed eastwards by the tribal allocation of Gad. They were frequently hostile to Israel and joined in alliances against her.
- Moab The Moabites were descended from Lot by his elder daughter. They were usually less hostile to Israel, and, rather than physically opposing the Exodus from Egypt, merely summoned the renowned Babylonian seer, Balaam to curse them, which God prevented him

The Antecedents of Two Faiths

from doing, his donkey being the victim of his frustration! The north-west part of their territory, which was to the east of the Dead Sea, was allocated to Reuben.

- Edom Edom is descended from Esau, and is thus more closely related than Moab and Ammon. Paul in Rom 9:6-13 confirms that the blessing of Abraham descends through Jacob and not through Esau, and emphasises what we noted earlier, namely that not all physical descendants of Jacob are spiritual descendants: *"For they are not all Israel, which are of Israel: Neither, because they are the seed of Abraham, are they all children: but, In Isaac shall thy seed be called"* (Rom 9:6-7). Edom means 'red', associated with Esau's complexion and his red stew. The whole of Genesis 36 is dedicated to his progeny. This is very complicated, especially as names were, as today, often duplicated. He and his family settled in the deeply dissected rocky country to the south east of the Dead Sea and in the valley south of that sea. They opposed the Children of Israel during the Exodus, despite a courteous request for right of passage with payment offered. *"And Moses sent messengers from Kadesh unto the king of Edom, Thus saith thy brother Israel, Thou knowest all the travail that hath befallen us"* (Numb 20:14). However being slightly more remote from central Israel, for at least three hundred years they caused no trouble. Amalek is listed among Esau's sons, but as the Amalekites were already a powerful race, it may be that this individual merely borrowed the name (see Numb 24:20). The entire little book of Obadiah is devoted to denouncing Edom, especially as, being descended from Isaac, she is counted by God as closer kin by a generation: *"And thy mighty men, O Teman, shall be dismayed, to the end that every one of the mount of Esau may be cut off by slaughter. For thy violence against **thy brother Jacob** shame shall cover thee, and thou shalt be cut off for ever"* (Obad 1:9-10). Interestingly. the Herods were of

Idumean or Edomite stock. On the other hand we are told In Mk 3:8 that Idumeans were among those who came to hear Jesus. Edom survived long as an entity, and in 536 AD was the see of a Christian Bishop!

As we shall see in the next chapter, some, but by no means all, of the above nations not only feature in the prophecies concerning what has long been history, but also in end-time events. Often a single prophecy contains a series of events which have been due to be fulfilled with long intervals between, and from the distant past to what is yet future. Read Psalm 83, which was written by Asaph almost three thousand years ago, and consider how much of it could have been penned last month. *"Keep not thou silence, O God: hold not thy peace, and be not still, O God. They have said, Come, and let us cut them off from being a nation; that the name of Israel may be no more in remembrance. For they have consulted together with one consent: they are confederate against thee: The tabernacles of Edom, and the Ishmaelites; of Moab, and the Hagarenes; Gebal, and Ammon, and Amalek; the Philistines with the inhabitants of Tyre; Assur also is joined with them: they have holpen the children of Lot.....Let them be confounded and troubled for ever; yea, let them be put to shame, and perish: That men may know that thou, whose name alone is JEHOVAH, art the most high over all the earth"* (Ps 83:1,4-8,17-18). We look again at this quote from Psalm 83 at 7.10. The Holy Spirit has ensured that these words were recorded to be read by every generation; and God has already sometimes intervened in judgment, without negating a future response on His part. Three of the Major and most of the Minor Prophets, including Post-Exilic, have singled out various of the perpetrators for warnings; a detailed synopsis may be found in Bill Randle's book, *A Sword on the Land* (see Bibliography).

CHAPTER FIVE

Jerusalem's Occupants in the Ichabod Age

*"Behold, your house is left unto you desolate.
For I say unto you, Ye shall not see me henceforth,
till ye shall say, Blessed is he that cometh
in the name of the Lord".*
(Matt 23:38-39)

5.1. JERUSALEM'S SIGNIFICANCE TO THREE FAITHS

To the modern Jew the famous Western Wailing Wall of the Temple Mount is the most sacred accessible point on earth, the former site of the Holy of Holies currently being inaccessible and its precise location by no means certain. Although Salem and Mount Moriah featured in Genesis with Melchizedek and with Abraham's sacrifice, Jerusalem did not become a Jewish city until the time when, *"The king and his men went to Jerusalem unto the Jebusites.... which spake unto David, saying..... thou shalt not come in hither..... Nevertheless David took the strong hold of Zion: the same is the city of David"* (II Sam 5:6-7). It became the permanent home of the Ark of the Covenant and the site of the Temple which God commissioned Solomon, rather than David, to build. The stronghold of Zion lay to the west side of the city and the Temple Mount to the east,

In the following section we shall quote other extracts from Solomon's dedication prayer; but note Solomon's plea: *"If they sin against thee.....and thou be angry with them, and deliver them to the enemy, so that they carry them away captives unto the land of the enemy, far or near; Yet if they shall bethink themselves in the land whither they were carried captives, and repent, and make supplication..... and pray unto thee toward their land, which thou gavest unto their fathers,* **the city which thou hast chosen, and the house which I have built for thy name***: Then hear thou their prayer and their supplication in heaven thy dwelling place, and maintain their cause"* (I Kings 8:46-49). This explains the longing of the exiles: *"By the rivers of Babylon, there we sat down, yea, we wept, when we remembered Zion..... If I forget thee, O Jerusalem, let my right hand forget her cunning. If I do not remember thee, let my tongue cleave to the roof of my mouth; if I prefer not Jerusalem above my chief joy"* (Ps 131:1,5-6). This reverence for his city explains why Daniel risked his Emperor's wrath and execution: *"He went into his house; and his windows being open in his chamber toward Jerusalem, he kneeled upon his knees three times a day, and prayed, and gave thanks before his God, as he did aforetime"* (Dan 6:10). Modern synagogues are built to face Jerusalem for the same reason.

To the Christian, especially the Gentile Christian, we are in the age and situation described to the Samaritan woman: *"Jesus saith unto her, Woman, believe me, the hour cometh, when ye shall neither in this mountain, nor yet at Jerusalem, worship the Father..... But the hour cometh, and now is, when the true worshippers shall worship the Father in spirit and in truth: for the Father seeketh such to worship him"* (Jn 4:21,23). Neither we Gentiles nor that woman have a covenant relationship involving Jerusalem; the hour had already come and now still is when we all must worship in spirit and in truth. In fact for many centuries this has also applied to the Jews, who did have such a covenant relationship, as much as the rest of us do. As we saw with Abraham in Chapter 4 and shall be reminded of in Chapter 6.5. and 6.6, the presence of a heavenly Jerusalem and the future descending New Jerusalem does not, as long as this earth shall remain, negate the legitimacy of the earthly city. Nevertheless, we should be very much aware of what the Bible tells us of

Israel in history and prophecy, or we will never be able to have a proper perspective of world events and how they relate to God's plan of the ages. It is not our place to advise God, who said to Jerusalem: *"For I know the thoughts that I think toward you, saith Jehovah, thoughts of peace, and not of evil, to give you **in your latter end** a hope..... and I will be found of you, saith Jehovah. And I will turn your captivity, and I will gather you from all the nations, and from all the places whither I have driven you, saith Jehovah; and **I will bring you again into the place whence I have caused you to be carried away captive"** (Jer 29:11,14 Dby). No Christian who cannot take at face value the poignant book of Hosea concerning Israel's past, present and unfulfilled future can style themselves as fully Bible believing.

The Muslim's position on Jerusalem is untenable. Randall Price records that in 1225 AD the noted Arab geographer Yakkut wrote that Jerusalem was holy to Jews and Christians, whereas Mecca was holy to Muslims. The fact is that it is chiefly because Muhammad's immediate followers recognised Jerusalem as the Holy City of the two faiths, which had the effrontery to reject his claims to be God's final prophet and refused to submit to Islam, that they sought to establish a bigger and better rival visible presence there. This has yet to be reversed, but in God's good time it will be. The true Islamic centres of worship are indeed Mecca and Medina. As we saw at 2.5., Muhammad's famous Night Journey was merely said to be from the Distant Shrine; it suited the personal ambitions of one early caliph to claim that this ascent was from the site of the Al Aqsar Mosque; and the myth has stuck, and during the past century much has been made of it. In fact, despite the fact that it was well known to Muhammad, the Koran never mentions Jerusalem by name in this or any other episode; it is much more likely that Medina, as opposed to Mecca, was meant as the distant shrine, and formerly Islamic scholars supported this. Indeed, for several centuries Mecca was regarded as the only Islamic shrine, and Islamic scholars denied that Jerusalem had any significance for them.

But modern Islam insists that the reference was to Jerusalem; thus in the 20th and 21st Centuries Muslims are told that it is the third holiest site in Islam – a splendid way to orchestrate international Islamic opposition to Judaism, which has much older and **very** much more thoroughly substantiated proofs of their claims to the city. Modern Islamic revisionism actually tries to deny the ancient Jewish presence, in very much the same way as the Holocaust has been denied in Germany. The Father of Lies is very active in this regard. The Mufti of Jerusalem, Sheik Ikrima Sabri, told the world that there was no indication whatsoever of any Jewish Temple having existed in Jerusalem; this is astonishing beyond belief, yet millions love to believe a lie. Quite apart from massive Christian and Jewish evidence, Babylonian, Greek, Imperial Roman and numerous other archeological and historical sources testify to both the existence and destruction of Jewish Jerusalem Temples.

It is paradoxical and mildly amusing that in February 2015 the Roman Catholics in Cordoba in Spain were accused of practising the same kind of revisionism, but in reverse, denying the Muslim foundation of that city's magnificent Islamic buildings. People calling themselves Christians simply must not give opportunities like this to the 'opposition'; we cannot counter lies with other lies.

5.2. ICHABOD – DEPARTED GLORY

The term 'Ichabod Age', as featured in the title of this chapter, does not occur in the Bible. However I trust that it will soon become clear why I am following the example of Baron and other Hebrew Christian scholars in using it.

In both Old and New Testaments, in other words long before Muhammad's time, Jerusalem is described as the Holy City, eg *"Bring one of ten to dwell in Jerusalem the **holy city**"* (Neh 11:1); *"Then the devil taketh him up into the **holy city**, and setteth him on a pinnacle of the temple"* (Matt 4:5). Note Jesus' description: *"I say unto you, Swear not at all; neither by heaven;*

for it is God's throne: Nor by the earth; for it is his footstool: neither by Jerusalem; for it is the city of the great King" (Matt 5:34-35).

Jerusalem is the city which God has chosen as His earthly dwelling place: *"And Jehovah the God of their fathers sent to them by his messengers..... because he had compassion on his people and on **his dwelling-place**"* (II Chron 36:15 Dby). Solomon, at the dedication of the first Jerusalem temple, prayed: *"that thine eyes may be open upon this house night and day, upon the place of which thou hast said, My name shall be there"* (I Kings 8:28-29 Dby). I shall frequently be using the Darby translation in this chapter too, because it does not substitute 'Lord' for the Name Jehovah, and Islam has long been determined to promote the name 'Allah' in the city of Jehovah. God said to Solomon: *"Since the day that I brought forth my people out of the land of Egypt I chose no city out of all the tribes of Israel to build a house in, that my name might be there; neither chose I any man to be prince over my people Israel: but I have chosen Jerusalem, that my name might be there"* (II Chron 6:5-6 Dby). There are numerous supporting texts. Although God has proclaimed and acted upon many promises of judgment, He has never withdrawn this statement.

So why has God allowed alien powers and individuals to occupy and to desecrate His city, and in particular His Jerusalem temple, which was once graced by His Shekinah glory? The answer is very simple. **Occupation** of the Land of Israel by the people of Israel has always been conditional; this was made very clear to them before they took **possession** of the Land under Joshua. The sad events of I Samuel chapter 4 are well known; God allowed the Ark of the Covenant to be taken from the Tabernacle by the Philistines, and the High Priest's newly born grandson was named *'Ichabod'*: *"She named the child Ichabod, saying, The glory is departed from Israel: because the ark of God was taken"* {Ichabod: that is, Where is the glory? or, There is no glory} (4:21-22).

That absence of the Ark was very short lived, because Dagon, the pagan god of the Philistines, was speedily humiliated by its presence. The Babylonian captivity lasted for seventy long years; *"For thus saith Jehovah: When seventy years shall be accomplished for Babylon I will visit you, and perform my good word toward you, in bringing you back to this place"* (Jer 29:10-11 Dby). The earlier part of Ezekiel, the account of the mighty prophet, who was one of the first to go into exile before Solomon's Temple was destroyed, is a major and too often neglected study in its own right; it tells us much that could be taken note of by apostate Christians. Let us look briefly at a few verses which remind us that exile is associated with abominations. Ezekiel's words were carried by various means to those who needed to hear: *"And mine eye shall not spare, neither will I have pity: I will render unto thee according to thy ways, and thine abominations shall be in the midst of thee; and ye shall know that it is I, Jehovah, that smite"* (Ezek 7:9 - Dby). The abominations, a relic of Nimrod's time, are recounted: *"And he brought me to the entry of the gate of **Jehovah's house** that was toward the north; and behold, there sat women weeping for Tammuz. And he said unto me, Seest thou, son of man? Thou shalt yet again see greater abominations than these. And he brought me into the inner court of Jehovah's house, and behold, at the entry of the temple of Jehovah, between the porch and the altar, were about five and twenty men, with their backs toward **the temple of Jehovah** and their faces toward the east; and they worshipped the sun toward the east"* (8:14-16 Dby).

5.3. THE DEPARTURE OF THE GLORY

During the Exodus the Children of Israel saw many manifestations of God's glory; but the one which was permanently visible only until the entry to Canaan was the miraculous pillar: *"the pillar of the cloud departed not from them by day, to lead them in the way; neither the pillar of fire by night, to shew them light, and the way wherein they should go"* (Neh 9:19). JM Riddle comments:

> "The pillar of cloud and fire was the emblem of divine defence and divine offence (Ex 14, 20,24). But pre-

eminently it was the symbol of his presence..... (Num 9:15-16). If the 'cloud' and 'fire' were literal before, then they will be literal again."

Thereafter, its guiding role having ended, it was rarely visible outside the Holy of Holies, which the High Priest entered only once a year; but God visibly demonstrated His presence in His Shekinah Glory at the dedication of the Temple: *"And it came to pass when the priests were come out of the holy place, that the cloud filled the house of Jehovah, and the priests could not stand to do their service because of the cloud; for the glory of Jehovah had filled the house of Jehovah"* (I Kings 8:10-11 Dby). In the following Ezekiel passages, the geographically distant prophet was permitted to see the departing glory, but the geographically nearby spiritually blind inhabitants could not.

David Baron, in his masterful 1901 work, writes:
"The words, Khebod Jehovah' (the glory of Jehovah), in the Hebrew scriptures always means the glory of the personal presence of Jehovah; the glory surrounding and attendant on the visible manifestations of Jehovah on the earth."

Usually, as noted, the Shekinah Glory was visible only to the High priest entering the Holy of Holies; but in vision it was made visible to Ezekiel. We read: *"And the glory of the God of Israel was gone up from the cherub, whereupon it was, to the threshold of the house"* (9:3). Sometime later we are told: *"And the cherubim lifted up their wings, and mounted up from the earth in my sight, when they went out; and the wheels were beside them; and they stood at the door of the east gate of Jehovah's house; and the glory of the God of Israel was over them above"* (10:19); and later still: *"And the cherubim lifted up their wings, and the wheels were beside them; and the glory of the God of Israel was over them above. And the glory of Jehovah went up from the midst of the city, and stood upon the mountain which is on the east side of the city"* (11:22-23). The Shekinah glory did not return to Jerusalem with the building of Nehemiah's Second Temple, and is not in fact due to return until the Millennium (Ezekiel 43), when mortals will not see the Lord in person after His visible Return in Power and the Judgment of the Nations.

Rabbi Youchanan has calculated that this glory was sitting upon the Mount of Olives for three and a half years, reluctant to leave. Baron reminds us of the three and a half years of our Lord's earthly ministry, when He was available to be recognised by His own. But at the end of that time, having unmistakably fulfilled the Great Halal (Psalms 113 to 118) and Zechariah's prophecy about His kingly coming upon an ass (9:9), He was rejected by the city. He cried out in Divine heartbreak: *"Ye shall not see me henceforth, **till ye shall say, Blessed is he that cometh in the name of the Lord"*** (Matt 23:39 KJV). The glory had been among them in the form of the Messiah Himself, fulfilling a multitude of Old Testament prophecies, but had been recognised by only the few: *"we beheld his glory, the glory as of the only begotten of the Father, full of grace and truth"* (Jn 1:14). Naturally the Lord would not appear at the same time in the form of the Shekinah Glory and as a Man. The veiled Glory was about to depart again. The nation's failure to recognise Him led to the second and longer phase of the 'Ichabod Age'; Heaven was about to receive Him *"**till the times of the restoring of all things**, of which God has spoken by the mouth of his holy prophets since time began"* (Acts 3:21 Dby). Thereafter during the Millennium, *"Jehovah will create over every dwelling-place of mount Zion, and over its convocations, a cloud by day and a smoke, and the brightness of a flame of fire by night: for over all the glory shall be a covering"* (Isa 4:5 Dby). That will be the evidence of His presence for mortals; but for immortal saints, *"They shall see his face; and his name shall be in their foreheads"* (Rev 22:4)

5.4. DISPERSAL AND CROWNLESSNESS
There is still light at the end of the tunnel for a nation which had to be scattered: *"And they shall know that I am Jehovah when I shall scatter them among the nations and disperse them through the countries"* (Ezek12:15 Dby). Not only Muslims, but recalcitrant Christians need to take note of a situation which is

of God's doing and is within strict time limits set by Him: *"Thou art become guilty by thy blood which thou hast shed, and hast defiled thyself with thine idols which thou hast made; and thou hast caused thy days to draw near, and art come unto thy years: therefore have I made thee a reproach unto the nations, and a mocking unto all countries"* (Ezek 22:4 Dby).

From the time of their return from Babylon to Christ's future Coming in Power there has never been, nor can there ever be, a king of David's line upon the throne in Jerusalem, although many imposters of other ancestries have usurped it. Even the Maccabees were not Davidic. *"And thou, profane, wicked prince of Israel, whose day is come, at the time of the iniquity of the end, --thus saith the Lord Jehovah: Remove the mitre and take off the crown; what is shall be no more. Exalt that which is low, and abase that which is high. I will overturn, overturn, overturn it! This also shall be no more, until he come whose right it is; and I will give it to him"* (Ezek 21:25-27 Dby): *"For the children of Israel shall abide many days without a king, and without a prince, and without a sacrifice, and without an image, and without an ephod, and without teraphim: Afterward shall the children of Israel return, and seek the LORD their God, and David their king; and shall fear the LORD and his goodness **in the latter days**"* (Hos 3:4-5).

The spiritual details revealed so graciously in the Book of Ezekiel give us an insight into what may have happened unreported at other times.

5.5. SUBSEQUENT DEFILEMENT OF THE JERUSALEM TEMPLE

Daniel prophesied of a coming vile usurper, the Seleucid Greek, Antiochus Epiphanes, who was to foreshadow the future Man of Sin, and who, in Apocryphal times, in 169 BC, plundered and desecrated the Temple, setting up a prototype Abomination of Desolation. But Jesus in His Olivet Discourse made it very clear that this desecration is to be repeated in the future (Matt 24:15,

Mk 13:14 – we will see more at 7.5.). Antiochus Epiphanes was five years later ousted by the heroic Maccabees.

In 37 BC Herod the Great captured Jerusalem and greatly enlarged and beautified Nehemiah's Post-Captivity temple, blasphemously claiming that in doing so he was fulfilling Haggai's Millennial prophecy (2:6-9) about the latter glory of the house being greater than the former. This of course was the Temple of Jesus' time on earth, and recognised by Him as His Father's House (Matt 21:13), also recorded by Mark and Luke. That was the temple, which the Romans under Titus destroyed in 70 AD, leading, as Jesus promised, to the great *diaspora*, dispersal or scattering, which has still not fully ended: *"and they shall fall by the edge of the sword, and shall be led away captive into all nations: and Jerusalem shall be trodden down of the Gentiles, **until the times of the Gentiles be fulfilled**"* (Lk 21:24) – and that 'Until, takes us beyond the demise of Islam.

In 136 AD The Roman Hadrian erected another abomination – the Aelia Capitolina, a temple to Jupiter on the Temple site, forbidding the few remaining Judean Jews to enter, not that many would have wished to do so.

Then in 330 AD the Byzantines, at least nominally Christian, occupied Jerusalem. They had no Scriptural commission to return to Jerusalem from which the preaching of the Gospel had begun (Acts 1:8), let alone to take possession of it. The time was not right for the great promised restoration of Israel or Jerusalem, which must await Messiah's return (Zech 14:4 etc, etc). Emperor Constantine's mother, Helena, and others did some very inefficient research and built magnificent Christian shrines, sometimes in quite the wrong places. To conform with Levitical law, Jesus' place of crucifixion and burial had to be outside the city and to the north; thus providentially the little hill which looks so like the "Place of a Skull" – Calvary – and the Garden Tomb are thankfully left unembellished, and visited by fewer tourists than the magnificent misplaced shrines. Constantine's son, Julian, reverted to paganism, and, under what was still the false impression that all Christians believed that God had no future purposes for the Jews, encouraged Jews to settle and even to plan a new temple in Jerusalem. The city was indeed rebuilt, as Muslims later discovered, but the Temple was not.

However after Julian's time the Temple Mount was turned by the Byzantines into a huge midden or dung heap, and it is recorded that so noxious was it that some suggested that this must be the prophesied Abomination of Desolation! They had become so preoccupied by the colossal Supercessionist or Replacement Theology lie stemming from Origen, Jerome and Augustine of Hippo, that God has forever abandoned Israel. This defilement of the Temple Mount, the place where God had put His name, was just one of the many follies perpetrated. The very early persecution of Christians by Jews had reaped its own rewards; it is important not to put all the blame on a single party, namely Islam, without considering all the factors.

In 614 AD the Persians conquered Jerusalem and destroyed many of the churches and Christian shrines, but in 629 AD Heraclius restored the city to Byzantine rule and rebuilt many of the churches. But the biggest and longest pagan occupation, the dominant one in the Ichabod Age, though one permitted by God, was just about to begin.

5.6. ISLAM – THE DOMINANT ICHABOD AGE PRESENCE

In 638 AD, only six years after the death of Muhammad, Caliph Umar Ibn Al-Maliq conquered Jerusalem. Islam was there to stay – for around thirteen hundred years excluding the Crusader occupations of 1099 to 1187 and 1229 to 1244 AD. The majority of Crusaders were quite as Anti-Semitic as the Muslims, and slaughtered as many Jews as Arabs. No enterprise so contrary to Scripture and therefore hateful to God could be expected to be blessed.

In addition to Arabs, the Egyptian Mamluks, Tartars and Mongols (the latter two being only superficially Muslim), and ultimately for four hundred years, the Ottomans were in occupation; all were Muslim. It is interesting that Umar chose the basilica of St Mary to pray, rather than some other Christian sanctuary, though whether this was because of its patronage or because it was at the southern extremity of the Temple Rock we do not know. It is a humiliating thought that he had to clear away a dunghill to free the site where sixty years later the first wooden Dome on the Rock (*Qubbat al-Sakhra*) was erected on the supposed place of Abraham's sacrifice.

Randall Price, whose excellent book "*The Battle of the Last Days Temple*", written in Jerusalem, examines these matters in great detail, remarks that much of the early Islamic building in Jerusalem, rather than being for strictly religious purposes, was to impress upon Christians and Jews the fact that they were now in charge and to convince them that Islam had replaced them; eventually their buildings were intended to outdo Christian ones in their magnificence. Muhammad had tried and failed to convince the Jews that he was God's ultimate prophet, whom they should accept; but Caliph Umar did his best to establish this myth in Jerusalem.

Although this is little known and even more rarely admitted, the first Al Aqsar mosque was a partial rebuilding of the Byzantine church erected by the Emperor Justinian. The neighbouring Dome on the Rock was built as a shrine, rather than as a mosque, and is liberally decorated with denouncements of Christian doctrine, as opposed to positive Islamic statements. While the two Muslim buildings, Mosque and Dome, are magnificent today, at various times they were damaged by earthquake and neglect and sometimes allowed to decay.

Through the centuries of the Islamic presence in Jerusalem, churches and other non-Islamic places of worship have been desecrated and occasionally plundered. In insolent defiance of

Christ's entry to Jerusalem on Palm Sunday and Ezekiel's as yet unfulfilled prophecy of the Messiah's return (43:4), a Muslim cemetery was opened outside the East facing Golden Gate to desecrate the site. By the 19th Century, with a weak Ottoman Empire and ascendant Europe, and with the Holy Land as a favourite tourist destination for the wealthy, Christian sites were not only comparatively safe, but many were expanded. Greek, Russian, Armenian, Coptic, Marionite, Ethiopian, Roman and even Protestant shrines brought the welcome prosperity, which Arabs were quick to cash in on, as many are to this day. With the support of wealthy Western Jews, Jewish settlements expanded.

5.7. PALESTINE, TRANSJORDAN AND ISRAEL

The Muslim Turks had joined the German side in the First World War. Although they successfully repelled British and allied attacks in Gallipoli near their heartland, they lost to the British, Australian, New Zealand and French forces all their remaining former imperial territory outside the present Turkish borders. On 19 December 1917 Field Marshall Lord Allenby took Jerusalem. As a Christian, aware of the future return of the true Messiah, he humbly dismounted from his horse and walked into Jerusalem via the Jaffa Gate when its Ottoman garrison surrendered. Whether or not they welcomed the fact that their liberator from four hundred years of oppressive Ottoman rule was a Christian, most of the inhabitants were happy initially about their new comparative freedom from neglectful Turkish colonialism. Great Britain took on the area then referred to loosely as Palestine, governing initially with a military administration, the boundaries being confirmed by the 1920 Franco-British Convention and Treaty of Sevres.

Five weeks before the capture of Jerusalem, the Balfour Declaration, in the form of a letter from the British Government to the Zionist Federation of Great Britain and Ireland via Rothschild, indicated Britain's favourable attitude to a Jewish homeland in 'Palestine', making it very clear that nothing should be done to prejudice the civil and religious rights of the existing non-Jewish population. This was of course in contrast to the attitudes for several centuries of that of the majority non-Jewish population to the civil and religious rights of resident non-Muslims!

The area between the Mediterranean and the Jordan continued to be known as Palestine, while the larger area east of the Jordan became Transjordan. This arrangement, having been ratified by the League of Nations on 24 July1922, came into force in September 1923. The provisions of the Balfour Declaration did not apply to Transjordan, and even in Palestine proved unworkable without a considerable British military presence to administer a sensitive balancing act between implacably hostile ethnic groups. There were separate Jewish and Muslim administrations and widespread segregation. However King Feisal of Transjordan welcomed the arrangement. After all, the unpopular Ottoman colonial power had been dismissed from the area, and the British role there was caretaker, rather than an imperial one. Feisal's words of welcome and cooperation to Zionist leader, Dr Weizmann, about Jews and Arabs being cousins are still on record.

Initially Palestine was a real patchwork quilt of territory, a fairly sparsely populated country with around 750,000 inhabitants, little irrigation and only subsistence agriculture. What is now the densely populated Gaza strip, a poverty stricken running sore of a territory, which rich Islamic nations were and still are content to leave that way, had, as recently as 1943, only one sizeable town, and even it had less than 30,000 inhabitants. Jewish immigration brought efficient irrigation and intensive agriculture and horticulture, mainly in *kibbutzim* collective communities, and within two decades the country was exporting vast quantities of food. Much of the land was purchased legally and permanently by the Jewish National Fund. Jerusalem was recognised as a Holy City of three faiths, and access, while not free from stress, was very much less restricted than after 1948, Muslims being able to profit handsomely from tourism to help ameliorate feelings of inter-faith rivalry and enmity.

Arab concern grew with the unforeseen rate of expansion of Jewish immigration, as the persecution of Jews increased in Central Europe. Eventually the Peel Commission had to report that "an irrepressible conflict has broken out between two national communities within the narrow bounds of one small country". As a young soldier, I met many officers and soldiers who wore the Palestine bar to their General Service Medal, and even the most devout Christians with sympathies towards the Jews admitted that it had been a most difficult and sensitive peace-keeping situation, with faults on both sides. When one reads Old Testament history, one should not be surprised! On 28th November 1941 the Grand Mufti of Jerusalem had an audience with Adolf Hitler, to make a covenant that the Arabs would give their support to Hitler's war on condition that, after annihilating Jews in Europe, Hitler would then abolish the Jewish Homeland in Palestine. Both assumed that Hitler would win the war; neither realised that the God, to whom they are ultimately answerable, once said: *"If those ordinances depart from before me, saith the LORD, then the seed of Israel also shall cease from being a nation before me for ever"* (Jer 31:36).

5.8. THE INTERIM SPIRITUAL SITUATION

Some hailed the 1917 Balfour Declaration as the end of the long Diaspora. And of course it would be wrong to say that it was not significant – the very beginning of what is proving to be a long drawn out end. Bible believing Christians were very excited at the 1948 birth of the State of Israel; I well remember listening avidly with my parents to the BBC news on the wireless (one did not talk about radios much) and reading my mother's *"Prophetic News".* The famous Israeli victories of 1967 and 1973 also caused much excitement, but in Christian circles mainly among those who took prophecy seriously; elsewhere in churches apathy was – dare one say 'rampant'?!

But spiritually Israel has yet to reach the end of the blindness, deafness and hardness of heart imposed in Isa 6:9-10, reinforced at Matt 13:14-15; Mk 8:17-18; Jn 12:38-41; Acts 28:26-27 and Rom 11:8. **Israel still languishes in an Ichabod condition.**

I now condense to a fraction of its former size Chapter 4 of my *"Christianity in a Global Crisis"*. In my *"Apocalypse Facts and Fantasies"* I devoted the much longer Chapters 3 and 4. These are very specifically 'untils' and not 'unlesses', but they do emphasise that until certain things happen, the Ichabod condition of the nation Israel will continue, and the presence of Pagans or apostates may be expected. Quotes in this section are from NKJV. Many of them are quoted as appropriate elsewhere in this book; here it is the 'untils' on which we focus:-

- Isaiah questioned God about the duration of the aforementioned hardness, blindness and deafness: *Then I said, 'Lord, how long?' and He answered: '**Until the cities are laid waste and without inhabitant**, the houses are without a man, the land is utterly desolate, and the Lord has removed men far away, and the forsaken places are many in the midst of the land. But yet a tenth will be in it, and will return and be for consuming, as a terebinth tree or as an oak, whose stump remains when it is cut down. So the holy seed shall be its stump.'"* (Isa 6:9-13). Even in exile God promised to preserve a remnant for national rebirth.
- In Romans 11 Paul says, *"God has given them a spirit of stupor, eyes that they should not see and ears that they should not hear, to this very day"* (v 8), and *"hardening of heart has happened to Israel **until the fullness of the Gentiles has come in**"* (v 25). Whether occupation has been by Roman, Byzantine, Christian or Muslims, the fullness of the Gentiles has yet to happen. Right now God has not completed the work that started just after Pentecost: *"God at the first did visit the Gentiles, to take from them a people for his name. And with this*

Jerusalem's Occupants in the Ichabod Age

the words of the prophets agree; as it is written, and I will build again the tabernacle of David, which is fallen down; and I will build again the ruins thereof, and I will set it up, that the residue of men might seek after the Lord". The fullness of the Gentiles is thus confirmed as following the completion of the Church and before the restoration on earth of Israel.

- *"For there will be great distress in the land and wrath upon this people. And they will fall by the edge of the sword, and be led away captive into all nations. **And Jerusalem will be trampled by Gentiles until the times of the Gentiles are fulfilled."*** (Lk 21:23-24). We will see in the next section how, within God's permissive will, this 'trampling' situation is still being preserved through the Muslim presence.

- It is of Jerusalem that Isaiah wrote: *"On the land of My people will come up thorns and briers..... because the palaces will be forsaken, the bustling city will be deserted..... **until the Spirit is poured upon us from on high**, and the wilderness becomes a fruitful field.... Then justice will dwell in the wilderness, and righteousness remain in the fruitful field. The work of righteousness will be peace, and the effect of righteousness, quietness and peace forever"* (Isa 32:13-17). Has this spiritual status been achieved within the Church Age? Most certainly it has not, even though much has been achieved. But God has promised, so it must happen. Verses too numerous to mention in major and minor prophets describe it.

- *"For Zion's sake I will not hold My peace, and for Jerusalem's sake **I will not rest, until her righteousness goes forth as brightness, and her salvation as a lamp that burns**. The Gentiles shall see your righteousness, and all kings your glory...... You shall also be a crown of glory in the hand of the Lord, and a royal diadem. You shall no longer be termed Forsaken, nor shall your land any more be termed Desolate..... I have set watchmen on your walls, O*

> *Jerusalem, who shall never hold their peace day and night. You who make mention of the Lord, do not keep silent, and **give Him no rest till He establishes and till He makes Jerusalem a praise in the earth**"* (Isa 62:1-4,6-7). No Gentile occupant will be able to resist God when His time comes, and all pagan and apostate relics having been forever removed.

- As He was about to be taken up to Heaven, Jesus was asked by the disciples, *"Lord, will You at this time restore the kingdom to Israel?"* (Acts 1:6). Later Peter, addressing his people, declared: *"Yet now, Brethren, I know that you did it in ignorance, as did also your rulers"* (3:17). Then he added: *"Repent then and be converted, that your sins may be blotted out, that times of refreshing may come from the presence of the Lord, and that He may send Jesus, who was preached to you before, **whom heaven must receive until the times of restoration of all things**, which God has spoken by the mouth of all His holy prophets since the world began* (Acts 3:19-21). Individual Jews were saved; the nation remained obdurate. God gave them a respite, but then declared: *"Therefore let it be known to you that the salvation of God has been sent to the Gentiles, and they will hear it!"* (Acts 28:28). The Gospel is still open to the Gentiles and the restoration of Jerusalem must await the return of the One Whom Heaven received. The present condition of Jerusalem, with its Muslim presence, conforms to Holy Scripture!

- The following passage has been quoted before, but must be repeated with the other 'untils' *"'O Jerusalem, Jerusalem, the one who kills the prophets and stones those who are sent to her! How often I wanted to gather your children together, as a hen gathers her chicken under her wings, but you were not willing! See! Your house is left to you desolate; for I say to you, **you shall see Me no more till you say, "Blessed is He who*** *comes in the name of the Lord!"'* (Matt 23:37-39). How pathetic is the diversionary excuse sometimes given, that references to Jerusalem after Acts refer to *'Jerusalem above'*. All the details given confirm that it is *'Jerusalem which is now, and is in bondage with her children'.* (Gal 4:25-26). This will be the culminating event of the future time when God makes Jerusalem an intoxicating *"cup of drunkenness to all the surrounding* (Arab) *peoples"* and *"Jerusalem a very heavy stone for all peoples; all who would heave it away will surely be cut to pieces, though all the nations of the world are gathered against it"* (Zech 12:2-3). We return to this at 7.8.

- We have already looked at this passage of Ezekiel: *"Now, to you, O profane, wicked prince of Israel, whose day has come, whose iniquity shall end, thus says the Lord God: 'Remove the turban, and take off the crown; nothing shall remain the same. Exalt the lowly, and abase the exalted. Overthrown, overthrown, and I will make it overthrown!* **It shall be no longer, until He comes whose right it is, and I will give it to Him.'"** (Ezek 21:26-27). And Jacob prophesied: **"The sceptre shall not depart from Judah, nor a lawgiver from between his feet, until Shiloh comes;** *and to Him shall be the obedience of the people"* (Gen 49:10). The rightful King of the Land and of Jerusalem is of Isaac's line through Judah, not of Ishmael's.

We have seen much evidence that the end of the Ichabod Age for Jerusalem still lies ahead, but is guaranteed by God. We need not be surprised by what has happened in Israel since the birth in 1897 of modern Zionism.

5.9. BIRTH OF A STATE BEFORE BIRTH OF A NATION

We now return to recent history. I have deliberately written "state" in contrast to "nation", because I believe that Isa 66:8-9 has been misapplied to events of May 1948, although certainly a nation state was constituted in a single day; but so were Yugoslavia, the Czech Republic and Slovakia! No. Isaiah prophesied of something miraculous, something unnatural: *"Who hath heard such a thing? who hath seen such things? Shall the earth be made to bring forth in one day? or shall a nation be born at once? for as soon as Zion travailed, she brought forth her children. Shall I bring to the birth, and not cause to bring forth? saith the LORD: shall I cause to bring forth, and shut the womb? saith thy God"* (Isa 66:8-9). I have to agree with WE Vine and JM Riddle that the travail, and therefore the birth, are still ahead; we will look at that in Chapter 7.10.

In 1939 a Westminster White Paper announced the limiting of Jewish immigration to 15,000 per year. The League of Nations was formerly disbanded in 1946, and the United Nations Organisation came into being. The British Post-War Labour government, with Ernest Bevin as Foreign Secretary, courted the friendship of the Arabs, and took an even tougher line than the Pre-War Government. Its attempts to achieve a settlement between Jews and Arabs was rejected by both sides, and on 14 February 1947 it ended the now obsolescent Mandate and handed the problem over to the United Nations. Humanly speaking Britain had been in an unenviable no-win situation. However in the Post-War years Britain derived no blessing from her ever less than enthusiastic part in the restoration of Jews to the Promised Land, particularly with her treatment of the pitiful Jewish refugee boat passengers. God had given her and her allies the victory over the Nazi perpetrators of perhaps the world's greatest Holocaust or 'Final Solution', and yet she was ambivalent in her admittedly difficult role. Who knows? Our nation's post-war economic and political recovery might have been less traumatic, had we honoured God in these matters.

The United Nations solution was partition, with international trusteeship for Jerusalem. The Jews reluctantly accepted the proposal, but the Arabs refused to cooperate in any way. However the **state** of Israel was born on 14 May 1948. I quote Dr Fred Tatford:

> "On 29 November 1947, the General Assembly of the United Nations adopted a resolution calling for the establishment of a Jewish State in the Land of Israel, and required the inhabitants themselves to take all measures necessary on their part to carry out the resolution. This recognition by the United Nations of the right of the Jewish people to establish their own State is irrevocable."

The Jewish territory consisted of three areas, namely Galilee west of the Jordan and Lake, most of the Mediterranean coast less the Gaza strip and a large Southern area, much of which was desert, coming to a sharp point at the port of Eilat on the Gulf of Aqaba. There were international crossing points at the two narrow 'waists' between these areas. It had a very short border with the City of Jerusalem, but enough to provide access, though running a gauntlet.

Within hours of the State being declared, it was invaded by the armies of Egypt, Iraq, Jordan, Lebanon, Saudi Arabia and Syria. As Dr Tatford comments:

> "To the amazement of the world, 650,000 Jews defeated the armies of over 40 million people."

By the time an armistice was signed in 1949, Israel, as the victim of aggression, had secured all of the inter-War period Palestine less what is now referred to as the West Bank, which was annexed by Jordan, leaving a comparatively narrow Jewish approach to Jerusalem. Jordan also took control of all of East Jerusalem with the Temple Mount and Mount of Olives, and kept this until the 1967 Six Days War. The Jordanian king denied Jewish access to the Wailing Wall, the focus of Jewish prayer since 70 AD. Eventually the PLO was given control.

5.10. RECENT YEARS

We simply cannot devote adequate space to the rivalry, hostility and conflict between Jew and Arab over the past six decades. But it is worthwhile mentioning that, following the overwhelming Israeli victory in the June 1967 Six Days War, it was widely expected in Islamic countries that East Jerusalem and the

Temple Mount in particular would be cleared of Islamic shrines and the Muslim population. Militarily it was a realistic option, and it could have been argued that, in view of the continued suppression of Jewish rights, it was morally acceptable to the international community, although some rabbis were afraid that they might inadvertently desecrate the site of the Holy of Holies. But the victorious Israeli Commander-in-Chief, Moshe Dayan, without Knesset authority, whilst securing access to the Wailing Wall, allowed the Jordanian agency to retain control of the Temple Mount, assuming wrongly that this remarkably generous concession would be regarded as an olive branch to peace. He should have known better; the Arabs were smarting too much to understand anything intended to be conciliatory. It was interpreted as weakness. However, in the light of Bible prophecy, we know that it was God Who overruled. We have already taken note of Jesus' Olivet Discourse prophecy of Lk 21:24: *"And Jerusalem will be trampled by Gentiles until the times of the Gentiles are fulfilled."* For reasons which we will see in our next two chapters, despite the **partial** end of the Diaspora, the Times of the Gentiles have yet to be fulfilled. The Gentile presence is due to remain a little longer, and is within God's plans as revealed in the Bible. We should never be afraid to emphasise that, whether to Jews, to fellow-Christians or to Muslims.

An understandable element in the Islamic militancy over the Temple Mount is the fact that it is widely known that there have long been Jewish plans afoot for the rebuilding of the Temple, whether on a completely cleared Temple Mount or in the space between the Al Aqsar Mosque and the Dome on the Rock. Most of the artefacts, materials and other necessities are ready, pending such a day. There is even an exhibition in Jerusalem, which I have seen, but not visited, publicising the project. Orthodox Jews are emphatic that no other location will conform to Levitical law. Yasser Arafat was very much aware of this and capitalised on its potential for agitation. Of course the Orthodox Jews, whose fathers rejected the Living Glory when He came to His Temple, know from several of the Prophets that there must one day be a magnificent Temple in Jerusalem to which the Glory of the Lord will return. But, as we will see at 7.5., the next one will not be the final one, but rather the place of the ultimate abomination.

In the meantime, throughout the Islamic world hatred towards Israel is being fanned to a white heat. Hatred is instilled from the cradle up, continuing throughout the education system as well as in the press and television. Hitler's *"Mein Kampf"* is prescribed reading in colleges, along with shamelessly distorted history books.

For those with open minds two sources of convincing proof of these lies are readily available: (1) Although it is rarely publicly acknowledged, Muslims within the state of Israel are not fleeing the land as refugees in the way that they are from some neighbouring Islamic lands; life there must have its advantages. (2) Despite the hatred and opposition taking so many forms, Israel has survived as a people for almost four thousand years, and is still surviving. Israel's God must not only be mighty, but Almighty; and that means He is Divine. There is much other evidence available to the thoughtful Muslim: *"For the wrath of God is revealed from heaven against all ungodliness and unrighteousness of men, who hold the truth in unrighteousness; Because that which may be known of God is manifest in them; for God hath shewed it unto them"* (Rom 1:18-19).

CHAPTER SIX

Contrasting Expectations

"Blessed and holy is he that hath part in the first resurrection: on such the second death hath no power".
(Rev 20:6)

6.1. THE COLLECTIVE AND INDIVIDUAL FUTURE

The title of this book is *"Israel, The Church and Islam, Past, Present and Future"*. Back in Chapter 1:11 we saw that the present time is the Acceptable Year of the Lord (Isa 61:2, Lk 4:19). It was announced by Jesus to His own people, Israel, at the start of His ministry; they rejected it, but it has continued throughout the Church Age and could end at any moment. Following the Rapture comes the Tribulation Period, involving the Day of Vengeance of our God (Isa 61:2; 63:4). Chapter 7 deals exclusively with that brief time; we will pay particular attention to what is likely to happen to Islam then, because after Christ's Return in power and glory at the end of the Tribulation Period comes the Millennium or Year of the Lord's Redeemed (Isa 63:4). We will see that Islam and all false religions will come to an end before the Millennium is ushered in. After the Millennium this world will pass away (Rev 21:1)., but that is not the 'end of the future' for humans; far from it.

In this chapter I wish to look at the future of individuals as well as the bodies or entities, namely Israel, Church or Islam, to which they belong. Being born an Orthodox Jew, Christian or Muslim does not mean that we have to die as one! *"For man goes to his eternal home, and the mourners go about the streets. Remember your Creator before the silver cord is loosed, or the golden bowl is broken, or the pitcher shattered at the fountain, or the wheel broken at the well. Then the dust will return to the earth as it was, and the spirit will return to God who gave it"* (Eccles 12:5-7 NKJV).

6.2. AFTERLIFE

By 'afterlife' I mean that which happens to the individual human after death. It has applied since the death of Abel, and should not be confused with eschatology, the doctrine of the last things. Like Judaism, Christianity and the ancient Persian monotheist religion, Zoroastrianism, which pre-dates Islam by two thousand years, Islam believes in Heaven and Hell, though as with Zoroastrianism and apostate Christianity, they are seen to be achieved by conduct during the former life.

Before going on in Chapter 7 to see how Islam might feature following the Rapture but before Armageddon, we must look at the contrasts between what the Bible, on the one hand. and the Koran and Hadiths, on the other, say about what happens to the individual after death. As a result of recent happenings, there is a growing and not unnatural understanding that some of the Jihadists assume that the greater the atrocities they commit, the more carnal for them Paradise will prove to be.

Once again it is imperative that we have a firm grasp of at least the basics of what the Bible teaches about the afterlife of the individual, because it is one of the many areas where Christianity and Islam are poles apart. Currently the differences come sharply into focus when Islam is so preoccupied with causing the deaths of those who oppose them, whether from within their own ranks or outside.

6.3. AFTERLIFE IN THE OLD TESTAMENT

In both the Old and New Testaments it is made abundantly clear that, until a great future day, there is to be an interval, in some cases of thousands of years, between death and the resurrection of the body and the reunification of what the New Testament teaches is the human trinity. OT saints were at least aware of the separation of the body and soul, although less aware of the distinction between spirit and soul.

Compared with the New Testament, not a lot of detail of the immediate afterlife is found in the Old Testament. In fact the expectation of the future resurrection is described more than the interim state of the soul and spirit. All the following verses assume this aforementioned interval between death and resurrection, and some confirm that the term 'sleep' is applied to the body rather than the soul. *"For I know that my redeemer liveth, and that he shall stand at the latter day upon the earth: And though after my skin worms destroy this body, yet in my flesh shall I see God: Whom I shall see for myself, and mine eyes shall behold, and not another; though my reins be consumed within me"* (Job 19:25-27); *"Thy dead men shall live, together with my dead body shall they arise. Awake and sing, ye that dwell in dust: for thy dew is as the dew of herbs, and the earth shall cast out the dead"* (Isa 26:19); *"And many of them that sleep in the dust of the earth shall awake, some to everlasting life, and some to shame and everlasting contempt. And they that be wise shall shine as the brightness of the firmament; and they that turn many to righteousness as the stars for ever and ever"* (Dan 12:2-3); *"In that day, saith the LORD of hosts, will I take thee, O Zerubbabel, my servant, the son of Shealtiel, saith the LORD, and will make thee as a signet: for I have chosen thee"* (Hag 2:23); *"And they shall be mine, saith Jehovah of hosts, in that day when I make up my jewels"* (Mal 3:17); *"But unto you that fear my name shall the Sun of righteousness arise with healing in his wings; and ye shall go forth, and grow up as calves of the stall"* (Mal 4:2).

As for the soul, in the Old Testament it is usually described as going to Sheol; the AV/KJV unhelpfully translates *sheol* thirty-one times as hell, thirty-one times as the grave and three times as the pit. In the Greek Septuagint they are consistently, and therefore helpfully, rendered as *hades*; (equally unhelpfully, in the AV New

Testament hades is translated ten times as hell and thirteen times as the grave). The 17th Century AV translators may have been trying to distinguish between *sheol* for the believer and *sheol* for the unbeliever, but that meant very subjective judgments, whereas sometimes there is no indication either way in the original. Before Christ's death, even the happier part of Sheol or Hades, *"Abraham's Bosom"* (Lk 16:2), the abode of the spirits of the believing dead awaiting the purchase of their redemption at Calvary, was **down**. When the witch of Endor was uniquely permitted to raise the spirit of Samuel for Saul, we read: *"And the king said to her, 'Do not be afraid. What did you see?' And the woman said to Saul, 'I saw a spirit ascending out of the earth'"* (I Sam 28:13). The Old Testament situation prevailed until Calvary. Thereafter it was **up**! Jesus, when He answered the thief, was going temporarily to **descend**, but the thief, with three hours of mortal life remaining, did not! Paradise moved that day!

Peter referred to the newly obsolete Old Testament situation of Pentecost, quoting Psalm 16: *"Him, ..., you have taken by lawless hands, have crucified, and put to death; whom God raised up, having loosed the pains of death, because it was not possible that He should be held by it..... **For You will not leave my soul in Hades**, nor will You allow Your Holy One to see corruption"* (Acts 2:23-24,27). Paul writes: *"When He ascended on high, He led captivity captive, and gave gifts to men." (Now this, "He ascended" --what does it mean but that He also first descended into the lower parts of the earth? He who descended is also the One who ascended far above all the heavens, that He might fill all things)"* (Eph 4:8-10).

6.4. THE FUTURE OF ISRAEL

Now we know that Satan must be a keen student of prophecy, and knows perfectly well that he can never alter what God has foretold as definite, but this does not stop him trying, because it is not in his nature to do otherwise. Muslims, on the basis of the Hadiths which so many of them believe, think that Islam will in due course destroy all Jews. Satan knows that it cannot, but continues to encourage those who think that they can. In fact, in different ways, he deceives both Jews and Muslims. During the first half of the Tribulation Period, as we will see at 7.6., he will deliberately preserve Israel for his own purposes, so that he can be worshipped in the Temple. However, once that has been achieved, he will wage such bitter war upon them, that God will commission and empower the Archangel to defend them (Dan 12:1).

Jewish believers from the Church Age will be resurrected or Raptured along with Gentile believers, and those from before the Church Age, or who die during the Tribulation will, as we have already noted, be resurrected about the time of Christ's Return in Power. Regarding the New Jerusalem we read that it *"had a wall great and high, and had twelve gates..... and names written thereon, which are the names of the twelve tribes of the children of Israel..... And the wall of the city had twelve foundations, and in them the names of the twelve apostles of the Lamb"* (Rev 21:12,14). Israel's identity is to be preserved throughout eternity.

We have seen that Israel has been side-lined for the duration of the Church Age, so, following the Rapture, the nation is due, over a period of a few years, to return to the 'mainline', and to the centre of God's purposes for the world. We read (the words in brackets are my comments): *"Simeon* (Simon Peter) *hath declared how God at the first did visit the Gentiles, to take out of them a people for his name* (the overwhelmingly Gentile Church). *And to this agree the words of the prophets; as it is written* (Amos 9:11-12), *after this* (after the Church has been completed) *I will return, and will build again the tabernacle of David, which is fallen down; and I will build again the ruins thereof, and I will set it up* (national restoration)*: that the residue of men might seek after the Lord, and all the Gentiles, upon whom my name is called, saith the Lord, who doeth all these things"* (Acts 15:14-17). Jerusalem is central to the Tribulation Period prophecies of Jesus' Olivet Discourse in Matthew 24, Mark 13 and Luke 21.

Contrasting Expectations

The Church is not mentioned there, not because Christ does not love His Church, but because she will be safe with Him in glory. It is Israel who will most need the warnings, as Satan's hatred is concentrated upon her in the absence of the Church (Rev 12:13,17).

It is to Jerusalem, to the Mount of Olives from which He departed, that Christ will return: *"Then shall the LORD go forth, and fight against those nations, as when he fought in the day of battle. And his feet shall stand in that day upon the mount of Olives"* (Zech 14:3-4). *"Behold, in those days, and in that time, when I shall bring again the captivity of Judah and Jerusalem, I will also gather all nations, and will bring them down into the valley of Jehoshaphat, and will plead with them there for my people and for my heritage Israel, whom they have scattered among the nations, and parted my land"* (Joel 3:1-2); *"And I will make them one nation in the land upon the mountains of Israel; and one king shall be king to them all: and they shall be no more two nations, neither shall they be divided into two kingdoms any more at all"* (Ezek 37:22); *"But in the last days it shall come to pass, that the mountain of the house of the LORD shall be established in the top of the mountains, and it shall be exalted above the hills; and people shall flow unto it. And many nations shall come, and say, Come, and let us go up to the mountain of the LORD, and to the house of the God of Jacob; and he will teach us of his ways, and we will walk in his paths: for the law shall go forth of Zion, and the word of the LORD from Jerusalem"* (Mic 4:1-2).

A vast choice of supporting scriptures is available; we live in a time of massive unbelief even within the Christian Church regarding God's unconditional promises for Israel. Even some born again Christians are inadvertently bringing temporary comfort to the Enemy and his servants, though in the long run that Enemy's dreadful fate is assured. For a thousand years Israel will at last enjoy the blessings conditionally offered in Moses' time in Deut 28:1-14, but forfeited through disobedience and sin for more than nineteen centuries, by their national rejection of their promised

Messiah, despite His having come with His credentials evident to all but the willingly blind, and forfeited even longer by those whose sin led to earlier captivities and exile.

Those of Israel, as well as a multitude of saved Gentiles, who, at the end of the Millennium, leave the Millennial earth in their mortal bodies, will become inhabitants of the New Earth (Rev 21:1), which, as we have seen, is to replace the old earth which is destined for destruction.

6.5. AFTERLIFE IN THE NEW TESTAMENT

On the evening of His arrest, Jesus reassured His own, once Judas had left the upper room: *"In my Father's house are many mansions: if it were not so, I would have told you. I go to prepare a place for you. And if I go and prepare a place for you, I will come again, and receive you unto myself; that where I am, there ye may be also"* (Jn 14:2-3) Better than 'mansions' are 'dwellings', 'dwelling places'; 'abiding places' and 'abodes'; some versions simply say 'rooms'. Jesus gave no hint that those abodes were yet in the future; **they existed already in His Father's House**; whereas **the place He was going to prepare was still future**. This distinction is too rarely understood. At death Church Age believers have not **yet** gone to the place He has gone to prepare, but to existing abodes or dwelling places within His Father's House.

We are not told specifically whom any other abodes are for, or whether Jesus was meaning that they were individual or collective. If collective, then we might consider that Church saints awaiting resurrection immediately prior to the Rapture are in one, and Old Testament saints, who **may** (there is some debate) have been described in Eph 4:18 as having been taken to Heaven at Christ's Ascension, are be in another, with their resurrection timed later at Christ's Return in Power: *"When he ascended up on high, he led captivity captive, and gave gifts unto men."* *"Captivity"* could be descriptive of Sheol which they had left. It is the liberty proclaimed to the captives of Isa 61:1.

Contrasting Expectations

Jesus' answer to the repentant thief tells us so much. He said to Jesus, *"'Lord, remember me when You come into Your **kingdom**.' And Jesus said to him, 'Assuredly, I say to you, **today** you will be with Me in Paradise.'"* (Lk 23:42-43). Whatever some cults teach to the contrary, the text is clear that they would be in Paradise that very day, He was not merely making the promise that day. Jesus did not explain that the hoped for Kingdom, which the thief (with remarkable faith in his agony) visualised, lay beyond the Church Age, although it does; He simply said that they would be together **that day** in Paradise, in other words within three hours, because the Jewish day ended at sunset, when all surviving victims had by law to be put to death. Yet their **lifeless bodies** would still be at or near the crucifixion site.

What Jesus had just accomplished was outside the realms of time as His body hung, shrouded in darkness, upon the cross. We simply do not know and cannot imagine how 'long' it seemed for our Lord's spirit and soul, before He could cry *"It is finished"*, as *"with His own blood He entered the Most Holy Place once for all"* (Heb 9:12). Almost three hours later, about sunset, when His **body** had been hastily laid to rest in a borrowed tomb, He was joined soul and spirit, **but not body,** in Paradise by the first true NT saint. Of course our Lord remained in Paradise only until His resurrection, when **His human trinity of spirit, soul and body were reunited**, as the Firstfruits of them that slept (I Cor 15:20). The thief still awaits his resurrection.

Even today, disembodied but fully conscious and at peace, Church saints await the main harvest of the First Resurrection at the Rapture for the espoused Bride. OT saints, who will be absent from the Marriage, but present at the Marriage Supper after the Lord's Return in Power, will have to wait a little until the slightly later gleanings, or final stage of the First Resurrection, following Christ's Coming in Power.

The glorious redemption of the body, true immortality, lies ahead for all believers. This does not in any way detract from the current joy and bliss of the *"dead in Christ"* (I Thess 4:16) *"For to me, to live is Christ, and to die is gain..... For I am hard pressed between the two, having a desire to depart and be with Christ, which is far better"* (Phil 1:21,23).

The place Jesus has gone to prepare is currently within the Father's House, waiting but unoccupied. It is **the bridal home**; it is for the resurrected and raptured saints complete in spirit, soul and body. When the Lord descends to the air, *"God will bring with Him those who sleep in Jesus"* (I Thess 4:14). When they return in their immortal bodies, from the aerial meeting place along with the newly raptured living believers, it will indeed be back to Heaven, but in a state and to a place within Heaven which they have not occupied before.

Believers, from the thief on, when they die, enter the Father's House individually. On a future glorious day the entire Church, the currently espoused Bride, whether resurrected or raptured, will enter the Prepared Place collectively. The Greek *'topon'* always means a place, a locality, room or similar, not merely a state or a condition. *"Then we which are alive and remain shall be caught up together with them in the clouds, to meet the Lord in the air: and so shall we **ever be with the Lord"*** (1 Thess 4:16-17).

Therefore we will be with our Lord **wherever** He is. Peter had seen Him received into Heaven. Later **He is going to leave Heaven** and descend in glory; and so must we! We have confirmation from Acts 3:20-21: *"Jesus Christ....**whom heaven must receive until** the times of restoration of all things."* That restoration we call the Millennium.

6.6. THE FUTURE OF THE CHURCH
Collectively, not individually, as we have seen, the Church is the espoused Bride of Christ (the 'Brides of Christ' ceremony observed in some churches was adapted from the pagan Roman Vestal Virgins and has nothing to do with Christianity).

Particularly in I Thess 4:17, we have identified the point where the futures of *"the dead in Christ"* and *"we who are alive and remain"* are to merge, and *"we shall ever be with the Lord."* Before the Marriage of the Lamb, but safe in Heaven, each individual must appear before the *Bema* or Judgment Seat of Christ, because the works done for Christ, which could **never** save us, have to be assessed: *"Every one of us shall give account of himself to God"* (Rom 14:12); *"For we must all appear before the judgment seat of Christ; that every one may receive the things done in his body, according to that he hath done, whether it be good or bad"* (II Cor 5:10); *"Lay up for yourselves treasures in heaven, where neither moth nor rust doth corrupt, and where thieves do not break through nor steal"* (Matt 6:20); *"Now if any man build upon this foundation gold, silver, precious stones, wood, hay, stubble; Every man's work shall be made manifest: for the day shall declare it, because it shall be revealed by fire; and the fire shall try every man's work of what sort it is. If any man's work abide which he hath built thereupon, he shall receive a reward. If any man's work shall be burned, he shall suffer loss: but he himself shall be saved; yet so as by fire"* (I Cor 3:12-15). Thus within the Body, the Bride of Christ, our personal level of honour is now being determined for all eternity – it is an incredibly solemn thought.

Once the entire Church is in Heaven and we have appeared at the *Bema*, the Marriage of the Lamb can take place – we are given no timescales for events in Heaven, but it is to be before Christ as the Bridegroom and King of Kings and Lord of Lords returns in power and great glory. *"Let us be glad and rejoice, and give honour to him: for the marriage of the Lamb is come, and his wife hath made herself ready. And to her was granted that she should be arrayed in fine linen, clean and white: for the fine linen is the righteousness of saints"* (Rev 19:7-8). *"And I saw heaven opened, and behold a white horse; and he that sat upon him was called Faithful and True, and in righteousness he doth judge and make war..... And **the armies which were in heaven followed him upon white horses, clothed in fine linen, white*** *and clean"* (Rev 19:11,14). Could it be that the horrified eyes of some Islamic executioner, having survived until Armageddon, will for a second divert his attention from the Rider of the white horse and spot in the *"armies which follow"* his former victim, risen and glorified?

The place our Saviour went to prepare so long ago is the eternal Holy City, New Jerusalem, where we shall *"ever be with the Lord"*. Evidently it is to descend at the beginning of the Millennium and be withdrawn following the Millennium, *"wherein the heavens being on fire shall be dissolved, and the elements shall melt with fervent heat"* (II Pet 3:12), also Rev 19:11: *"And he carried me away in the spirit to a great and high mountain, and shewed me that great city, the holy Jerusalem, descending out of heaven from God"* (Rev 21:10); *"And I John saw the holy city, new Jerusalem, coming down from God out of heaven, prepared as a bride adorned for her husband"* (Rev 21:2). Exactly how the New Jerusalem and Millennial earth will relate to each other we cannot yet say precisely, except that it will be a very close relationship, because immortal saints will have delegated authority on earth, so must have ready access: *"Verily I say unto you, That ye which have followed me, in the regeneration when the Son of man shall sit in the throne of his glory, ye also shall sit upon twelve thrones, judging the twelve tribes of Israel"* (Matt 19:28); to the little congregation or assembly at Thyatira He said: *"He that overcometh, and keepeth my works unto the end, to him will I give power over the nations"* (Rev 2:26. I have dealt with these matters in considerable detail in *"The Millennium – Restoration After Retribution"*. Such is the glorious future of the Church.

6.7. AFTERLIFE IN THE KORAN AND ISLAMIC TRADITION

The afterlife in Islam is known as *akhira* and is taken seriously. This teaching is not as dissimilar to ours as those Eastern religions which believe in an endless and hopeless cycle of transmigration, in which the way in which one behaves during one life will determine whether one returns in the next as an elephant,

Contrasting Expectations

a monkey, an oyster or dung beetle or even another human. Nevertheless Islamic afterlife teaching is more akin to Greek mythology than to either Jewish or Christian. Now admittedly Allah is not included here, because he is never claimed to have been mortal; but the conditions and behaviour predicted in Islam for those who were once mortal and have entered immortality after death are not unlike what was supposed to happen among the Olympian gods and goddesses, where immortals indulged in similar activities to mortals, but on a much grander scale and with more fantastic results. Sin for the Olympians was generally practised with impunity, although there was always the chance that one might be transformed into something picturesque or grotesque, but no longer human, if one offended someone more influential than oneself.

Paradise in Islamic teaching, is in reality an extension of Cain's religion, a reward, not a blood-bought gift: *"As for those who believed and did righteous deeds, for them will be the Garden of Refuge as accommodation for what they used to do"* (Surah 32:19). In the Koran those destined for Paradise have their records in their right hands, and those destined for Hell in their left. In Surah 56 we read: *"Those are the ones brought near [to Allah] in the gardens of pleasure, a [large] company of the former peoples and a few of the later peoples on thrones woven [with ornaments], reclining on them, facing each other. There will circulate among them young boys made eternal with vessels, pitchers and a cup [of wine] from a flowing spring – no headache will they have therefrom, nor will they be intoxicated – and fruit of what they select and meat of fowl, from whatsoever they desire. And [for them are] fair women with large [beautiful] eyes, the likeness of pearls well protected, for reward for what they used to do"* (vv 11-24)….. *"And [upon] beds raised high. Indeed we have produced them [i.e. the woman of Paradise] in a [new] creation and made them virgins, devoted [to their husbands] and of equal age."* (vv 34-37). What an incredibly sexist place the Islamic paradise purports to be – but free from hangovers! Muhammad's imagination could only stretch as far as a celestial harem which would satisfy his own appetites. Tragically this is what the male suicide martyrs expect, and those clerics who encourage them seem not to indicate any long delay till the day of judgment for all the above, although other passages of the Koran do suggest an interval between death and resurrection. Surah 88:8-16 also describes Heaven and Hell, but without further mention of the physical extravagences.

When questioned by the Sadducees, Jesus Christ, with unassailable authority, said *"Ye do err, not knowing the scriptures, nor the power of God. For in the resurrection they neither marry, nor are given in marriage, but are as the angels of God in heaven"* (Matt 22:29-30). Would some of the mullahs who send some of their followers to gruesome deaths only listen to the One who came from Heaven - the One Who knows the truth. Few if any of these mullahs seem to be anxious to die themselves.

The Bible teaches that all will rise at either the First Resurrection or the Second. But Muslims believe the immortal resurrection body to be to similar specifications as the former mortal body, right down to fingerprints: *"Does man think We will not assemble his bones? Yes. [We are] able to proportion his fingertips"* (Surah 75:3-4). They interpret Surah 32:10 as condemning those who cannot believe this: "*And they say, 'When we are lost [i.e.disintegrated] within the earth, will we indeed be [recreated] in a new creation. Rather they are, in the meeting with their Lord, disbelievers."* This is all in contrast with Bible teaching: *"There are also celestial bodies, and bodies terrestrial: but the glory of the celestial is one, and the glory of the terrestrial is another..... It is sown a natural body; it is raised a spiritual body"* (I Cor 15:40,44); *"As was the man of dust, so also are those who are made of dust; and as is the heavenly Man, so also are those who are heavenly. And as we have borne the image of the man of dust, we shall also bear the image of the heavenly Man"* (I Cor 15:48-49 NKJV).

Islam teaches a sort of second chance Purgatory, although

Contrasting Expectations

it seems that only a minority are expected to pass that test successfully: *"And we will let them taste the nearer punishment short of the greater punishment that perhaps they will return [i.e. repent]."* The Bible, of course, teaches no such second chance after death, although apostate Christians whom Muhammad met probably did believe in Purgatory. I Cor 3:15, often quoted to support Purgatory, is about works being burned, not people.

Islamic teaching gives a dangerous deathbed reassurance: "Whoever's last words are, *'There is no God but Allah'* will enter Paradise. The source is Hadith rather than Koran. This is of course a negative statement or formula which is supposed to guarantee access to Heaven; most Muslims will wish to die with these words on their lips and relations are encouraged to facilitate this – which of course is reasonable and commendable, *were the formula to be valid*. What a way to gain Paradise! It is hardly necessary to comment that **this naming of Allah rules out all other names**. As Christians we are reminded: *"Jesus Christ of Nazareth......There is none other name under heaven given among men, whereby we **must** be saved"* (Acts 4:10,12). The *"can be saved"* of the NIV is too weak; Young's Literal Translation says: *"in which it behoveth us to be saved"*. Paul writes: *"No man can say that Jesus is the Lord, but by the Holy Ghost"* (I Cor 12:3). The context makes it clear that this confession is no mere recitation or formula, and that it is the work of the Spirit of God, and acceptance of that Name which means Saviour.

The Islamic deathbed is to be turned if possible towards Mecca to facilitate prayer. Incredibly complex rituals are dictated for shrouding of the deceased, except martyrs who are usually buried "with their blood" in the clothes in which they met their death.

Hell in Islam shares various features with Hell or Gehenna in the Bible, and, as in the Bible (Rev 20:5,12), their bodies are to be resurrected to face it. However, novel is the idea that the damned are to be led to Hell by the Pharaoh of Moses' day: *"He will precede his people on the Day of Resurrection and lead them into the Fire; and wretched is the place to which they are led"* (Surah 11:98); *"[They will be] in scorching fire and scalding water and a shade of black smoke"* (Surah 56:42-43); *"But if he was of the deniers [who were astray]. Then [for him is] accommodation of scalding water and burning Hellfire. Indeed this is the true certainty"* (Surah 56:93-95). Elsewhere the craving for water is likened to that of a thirsty camel.

The Bible tells us that Hell, as opposed to Sheol or Hades, will not be inhabited by any human until this creation has passed away: *"And I saw a great white throne, and him that sat on it, from whose face the earth and the heaven fled away; and there was found no place for them..... And whosoever was not found written in the book of life was cast into the lake of fire"* (Rev 20:11,15). The Koran tells us: *"[They will be] abiding therein as long as the heavens and the earth endure, except what your Lord should will"* (Surah 11:107). This is interpreted as saying that a few may eventually be reprieved.

Throughout these accounts of Islamic afterlife one is frequently reminded that Muhammad had been aware of the Jewish and Christian traditions, which initially he had hoped to modify into his new 'revelation'. It is, to put it bluntly, one man's attempt, not so much to nullify, but rather to improve upon what God's Holy Spirit had already revealed. Superficially it may appear plausible; but in fact it amounts to blasphemy. When Peter tried to improve upon his Lord's plans, Jesus *"turned, and said unto Peter, Get thee behind me, Satan: thou art an offence unto me: for thou savourest not the things that be of God, but those that be of men"* (Matt 16:23). We are reminded of the ancient Manipulator and Distorter of God's words, who started his nefarious activity on earth back in Eden, and is still incredibly busy.

6.8. THE FUTURE OF ISLAM

I have approached the previous two sections on Israel and the Church with confidence, knowing that I am in broad agreement with those other commentators who hold the predictive prophecy of the Bible in high regard; I know that Scriptural support is massive. But in this section I can simply draw a few conclusions about Islam based on what we will be seeing in chapter 7.4., namely why Islam is likely to be jettisoned by the Beast and his ten kings along with all other religions ancient and modern, other than, perhaps, the few which have been overtly Satanic.

With incredible effrontery Muhammad set himself up as a greater than Moses and even claimed to be greater than Jesus Christ. He has led millions in his erroneous ways, and been responsible for more bloodshed than any religious leader in the world's history – and competition has been pretty fierce, including some who have claimed to be Christians. So with a record of blasphemy like that, even if Islam survives the Beginning of Sorrows, it seems certain that it cannot survive the Great Tribulation.

However, before we write off Muslims in the Tribulation, we should consider and learn from a prophecy which refers to the Millennium, but reflects what will have happened earlier during the Tribulation Period: *"And Jehovah will smite Egypt; he will smite and heal: and they shall return to Jehovah, and he will be entreated of them, and will heal them. In that day shall there be a highway out of Egypt to Assyria; and the Assyrian shall come into Egypt, and the Egyptian into Assyria; and Egypt shall serve with Assyria. In that day shall Israel be the third with Egypt and with Assyria, a blessing in the midst of the earth; whom Jehovah of hosts will bless, saying, Blessed be Egypt my people, and Assyria the work of my hands, and Israel mine inheritance!"* (Isa 19:22-25 Dby). Again I use Darby's translation to emphasise that God is using His covenant Name where we might not have expected it. It is very clear from the Judgment of the Nations, which, unlike two proceeding parables, is presented as straightforward prophecy, that only saved survivors of the

Great Tribulation will enter the Millennial Kingdom: *"When the Son of man shall come in his glory, and all the holy angels with him, then shall he sit upon the throne of his glory: And before him shall be gathered all nations: and he shall separate them one from another, as a shepherd divideth his sheep from the goats..... Then shall the King say unto them on his right hand, Come, ye blessed of my Father, inherit the kingdom prepared for you from the foundation of the ..... Then shall he say also unto them on the left hand, Depart from me, ye cursed, into everlasting fire, prepared for the devil and his angels"* (Matt 25:31-32,34,41). This indicates that great numbers of both Assyrians and Egyptians are going to hear the Gospel of the Kingdom during the Tribulation Period and will be saved.

If this is true, and it evidently is, there is no reason to believe that many from the Ishmaelite nations will turn to Christ and be saved during the same period; but apparently their **nations** will not survive to take their place on the Millennial earth. This is incredibly good news for individual latter day Muslims, though few would acknowledge it yet. Once children are born to the Egyptians, Assyrians and other Millennial nations, they will be required to acknowledge and worship: *"And it shall come to pass, that every one that is left of all the nations which came against Jerusalem shall even go up from year to year to worship the King, the LORD of hosts, and to keep the feast of tabernacles. And it shall be, that whoso will not come up of all the families of the earth unto Jerusalem to worship the King, the LORD of hosts, even upon them shall be no rain. And if the family of Egypt go not up, and come not, that have no rain; there shall be the plague, wherewith the LORD will smite the heathen that come not up to keep the feast of tabernacles. This shall be the punishment of Egypt, and the punishment of all nations that come not up to keep the feast of tabernacles"* (Zech 14:16-19). We are again reminded that the Millennial earth is no picture of Heaven, but a last chapter in the history of this old world. The Tempter will be securely bound in the Abyss or Bottomless Pit (Rev 20:3).

6.9. NO ISLAMIC MILLENNIAL TEACHING

The previous paragraph took us to the Millennium. Glasson writes about the decline of teaching of Millennialism or Chiliasm in the early Church (I have dealt with these matters in considerable length in *'Apocalypse Facts and Fantasies'* and *'The Millennium – Restoration After Retribution'*).

> "The final collapse of chiliasm, as far as the main Christian tradition was concerned, was due to St Augustine, the famous Bishop of Hippo in North Africa, who lived from 354 to 430. He was responsible more than anyone else for popularising the view that we are now living in the millennium...... He writes: 'He that looks for great good in this world, is far wrong. The place therefore where this promised peace will dwell and abide is the heavenly Jerusalem.'"

This is one of the most subtle attacks on Holy Scripture, because people are thus compelled to see a variety of prophecies as inconsistent and sometimes contradictory pictures of Heaven. This would be what Muhammad would have met among Christians. False teaching can have much greater and longer lasting repercussions than we imagine.

The most that modern followers of Muhammad hope for before death or before the *Day of Recompense* at the end of the world is 'Islamisation', or universal total submission to Allah through the efforts of Islam, in very much the way that Post-Millennialists hope for a 'Christianised' world through the Church's efforts before Christ's personal intervention. The Bible in contrast foretells for **this planet** what many Christians and many Muslims see as pictures of Heaven: the physical attributes are found in such lovely passages as *"The wolf also shall dwell with the lamb, and the leopard shall lie down with the kid; and the calf and the young lion and the fatling together; and a little child shall lead them..... They shall not hurt nor destroy in all my holy mountain: for **the earth** shall be full of the knowledge of the LORD, as the waters cover the sea"* (Isa 11:6,9); *"The wilderness and the solitary place shall be glad for them; and the desert shall* *rejoice, and blossom as the rose..... Say to them that are of a fearful heart, Be strong, fear not: **behold, your God will come with vengeance, even God with a recompence; he will come and save you"** *(Isa 35:1,4); *"And they shall build houses, and inhabit them; and they shall plant vineyards, and eat the fruit of them. They shall not build, and another inhabit; they shall not plant, and another eat: for as the days of a tree are the days of my people, and mine elect shall long enjoy the work of their hands"* (Isa 65:21-22). Zechariah chapter 8 from v 3 is too long to quote, but is most instructive.

What is of course anathema to most Muslims, is that in the Bible a restored Jerusalem features prominently in the Millennial earth; but there are Christians to whom this is anathema too. But praise the Lord! Both Muslims and nominal Christians are still coming to a saving faith in the Lord Jesus Christ, and some are prepared to take the Bible at face value, when it says *"And Jehovah shall be king over all the earth: in that day shall there be one Jehovah, and his name one"* (Zech 14:9 Dby). This is future but clearly before the end of the world.

Can anything be clearer, that these are prophecies and not pictures, and follow rather than precede Christ's Second Coming in Power? What Muslims need to observe is that what some Christians taught in Muhammad's time, which he modified to suit his own personal tastes, is not of what the Bible teaches about Heaven, but rather about mortals during the Millennium. What we have to concede is that the aspirations and expectations of Muslims match on the whole what the Koran teaches more than many Christians' aspirations and expectations match Bible prophecy.

In the meantime we can be assured that the Millennium is still some way ahead beyond earth's greatest trials: *"The Lord said to My Lord, 'Sit at My right hand **till I make Your enemies Your footstool.'** The Lord shall send the rod of Your strength out of Zion. Rule in the midst of Your enemies"* (Ps 110:1-2). We are

Contrasting Expectations

left in no doubt as to where Jesus Christ is at present. *"I also overcame and sat down with My Father on His throne"* (Rev 3:21). He will remain in Heaven until He goes forth to wage war against His enemies, and to rule with a rod of iron (Rev 19:15). When, without warning and before earth's darkest hour since the Flood, He comes for His Church to take us to the place He has gone to prepare, the glorious meeting will be no further than Heaven's visible cloudy threshold.

CHAPTER SEVEN

The Demise of Ancient Religions And Feuding Nations

"The seventh angel sounded; and there were great voices in heaven, saying, The kingdoms of this world are become the kingdoms of our Lord, and of his Christ; and he shall reign for ever and ever" (Rev 11:15).

7.1 ISRAEL AND ISLAM IN THE TRIBULATION PERIOD

We now turn our attention to the period between the Rapture of the Church and the Return of the Lord Jesus Christ in power and glory. We have already referred to it as the Tribulation Period. We are not told exactly how long it will last, but can say that it is to be dominated by a seven year period which will be explained more fully at section 7.5. However it cannot begin until the next prophetically recorded event on earth has taken place. The redeemed saints are seen raptured or resurrected in Heaven (Revelation chapters 4 and 5). Jesus Christ in His offices of the *"Lion of the tribe of Judah, the Root of David"* and the *"Lamb as it had been slain"* (Rev 5:5-6) opens the first of seven seals of a scroll, and the first 'horseman of the apocalypse' introduces or authorises the start of the career of the Beast who will impose the seven year covenant of Dan 9:27: *"And behold a white horse: and he that sat on him had a bow; and a crown was given unto him: and he went forth conquering, and to conquer"* (Rev 6:2). Those seven years will be divided equally into the Beginning of Sorrows and the Great Tribulation or Time of Jacob's Trouble. We are looking at these matters chiefly in connection with the ancient enmity between the seed of Jacob (Israel) and that of

Ishmael, and what the Bible indicates is to happen to Islam, and how this compares with Islamic expectations.

7.2. ISLAMIC END-TIME PROPHECY

While it is God, not Allah, who knows the future. and who allows nothing to be done outside His sovereign will, it is essential in any debate to know the end-time expectations and aspirations of Muslims, which explain much that is a mystery to others. The Islamic Hadiths, of which there are several versions varying in prophetic sequences and other details, teach that the last hour will not come until ten signs have been fulfilled. These include:-

- The *Dajjal*, equating roughly to the Bible's Man of Sin (II Thess 2:3) or First Beast (Rev 13:1-10), the Little Horn of Dan 7:20 and the Wilful King of Dan 11:36 etc.
- The Beast from the Earth, equating in some respects with the Bible's Second Beast (Rev 13:11-18) or False Prophet. See section 6.4. for this and the previous bullet point.
- The descent of Aisa, Son of Miriam; much less spectacular than in the Bible, but equating in some respects to the Second Coming in Power of the Lord Jesus Christ, (cf Zech 14:4, Matt 24:27-30, Mk 13:26, Rev 1:7, Rev 19:11-16, etc). He is said to destroy both the Dajjal (see Rev 19:20) and the Jews. But in studying his claimed activities, this Islamic Aisa is no nearer to being the Jesus of the Bible than the Islamic Miriam is to being the lovely humble mother described in the Gospels.
- Gog and Magog - The Bible talks of *Gog of the land of Magog* in Ezek 38:2, and devotes Ezekiel chapters 38-39 to his disastrous defeat. Gog and Magog are involved in a separate end-of-the-world prophecy at Rev 20:7-9. The Hadith accounts compare much more with the Ezekiel prophecy than the Revelation one. Section 7.7. is devoted to this..
- Massive escalation of slaughter, (cf Matt 24:22, Rev 6:12, Rev 9:15).

- The sun rising in the West, instead of the East; there is no direct Bible equivalent, though the sun standing still in Joshua's victory over the Amorites (Josh 10:12-13) and the shadow of the sun returning ten degrees in Hezekiah's time (II Kings 12:9-11) might be seen as precedents, while Zech 14:7 tells of a less clearly specified phenomenon, probably extended daylight, on the day that Christ returns to the Mount of Olives.
- Massive earthquakes, all in the Middle East but varying in location, cf Isa 11:15, Isa 24:19-20, Zech 14:4-5, Matt 24:7, Rev 6:12; 16:18-20
- The *Al-Fitan* – a time of trials and affliction – compare with the Great Tribulation (Dan 12:1, Matt 24:31, Rev 7:14). Much of this chapter deals with this, but in particular sections 7.8. onwards.

The comparable Bible references are far from exhaustive. It will immediately be obvious to anybody familiar with Christianity that most of the above are Islamic developments or corruptions of Bible prophecies. Not surprisingly, none escapes massive Islamic amendment. Yet some of the similarities between the Islamic end-time prophecies and Bible ones are striking, even if the outcomes are **very different as to whom they favour, usually being the reverse of the Bible original**. Again one senses the influence of some higher intelligence with a personal axe to grind and an acute awareness of Bible prophecy. The evidence that the Bible prophecies are the earlier ones is beyond dispute. For instance, every one of the Old Testament references listed above can be found in the 2nd Century BC Greek Septuagint version, which exists intact.

Some Christians are put to shame by the strength of Islamic enthusiasm for the arrival of the Mahdi, or Muhammad al-Mahdi, Muhammad ibn Hasan or the Twelfth Imam compared to limited enthusiasm for our Lord's Return within so many churches. The Twelfth Imam is seen as a sort of Islamic Messiah, a descendant of the Prophet's family, whose precise time of arrival seems to vary from Hadith to Hadith, but fits somewhere into their end-time expectations. Sunnis do not dismiss him entirely, though they are more cautious, because he does not feature prominently in the Koran. Among many Shi-ites he is supposed to have been secreted more than a thousand years ago by Allah in a Persian well, when still a boy, in a state of suspended animation, awaiting the Day of Judgment, when he will be summonsed by Allah. Some say that he will return with A'isa Son of Miriam (Jesus the Son of Mary) to proclaim that Islam is the true faith and rid the world of evil, and rule in peace and equity for either seven, nine or nineteen years (depending on which Hadith one reads) before the end of the world! Jesus is supposed to return to be married and have children and eventually die the death which Muhammad claimed He did not die before!!!

The present turbulent situation between Islamic states and Israel is thought to be a sign of the nearness of these events. Again many Christians stand condemned, when one considers how current events are seen to be outside the scope of Bible prophecy, which Preterists think of as having run out of steam nearly twenty centuries ago. Muslims may thus be led to think that Allah has entrusted them with more information than our God has in the Bible. It is a dreadful indictment on current Christian commitment to Bible truth.

7.3. THE TRINITY OF EVIL
This and the following three sections should be read before we will be in position to give an opinion on the future of Islam **as a religion** after the Rapture. From section 7.7. we can examine the end-time role of what are currently Islamic nations. When dealing with Satan and his hosts, we should remember that each one of us is vulnerable and that we can overcome only by the blood of the Lamb (Rev 12:11); even the Archangel was cautious (Jude 1:9) and holy angels have their battles. The evil angelic prince with delegated responsibility for Persia in prophesied matters was able to resist God's holy angel for several weeks – an intriguing disclosure in view of current events (Dan 10:13-

15). However there is a strict limit to how much Satan can harm any blood-bought believer.

The short interval between the Rapture and Christ's Return in Power is usually referred to as the Tribulation Period. It will be Satan's last desperate bid for universal worship in a rebellion that started before the creation: *"Thou art the anointed cherub that covereth; and I have set thee so: thou wast upon the holy mountain of God; thou hast walked up and down in the midst of the stones of fire. Thou wast perfect in thy ways from the day that thou wast created, till iniquity was found in thee"* (Ezek 28:14-15); *"Thou hast said in thine heart, I will ascend into heaven, I will exalt my throne above the stars of God: I will sit also upon the mount of the congregation, in the sides of the north: I will ascend above the heights of the clouds; I will be like the most High. Yet thou shalt be brought down to hell, to the sides of the pit"* (Isa 14:12-15).

The nearest Satan is ever going to be able to achieve his ambitions on this planet will be around the mid-point of the Tribulation Period, and is described in II Thess 2:3-4: *"Let no man deceive you by any means: for that day shall not come, except there come a falling away first, and that man of sin be revealed, the son of perdition; Who opposeth and exalteth himself above all that is called God, or that is worshipped; so that he as God sitteth in the temple of God, shewing himself that he is God"*. This will take the form of the one who has been aptly described as the third person of the Trinity of Evil directing the world's worship and adoration through the First Beast to his Satanic master in a parody of the Holy Trinity. Later they will precede him into the Lake of Fire (Rev 19:20).

Satan, as already noted, will during the Tribulation Period have two human representatives and deputies, the Beast and False Prophet. The Second Beast or False Prophet is apparently not to be made public until the mid-point of the seven years, when Satan, also described as the Dragon, has been deprived of his last privileges: *"Rejoice, ye heavens, and ye that dwell in them. Woe to the inhabiters of the earth and of the sea! for the devil is come down unto you, having great wrath, because he knoweth that he hath but a short time"* (Rev 12:12); *"And I beheld another beast coming up out of the earth; and he had two horns like a lamb, and he spake as a dragon. And he exerciseth all the power of the first beast before him, and causeth the earth and them which dwell therein to worship the first beast, whose deadly wound was healed"* (Rev 13:11-12). Obsolete, as we will see in our next section, will be the worship of the ancient multi-faith Mystery; public will be the worship of Satan's avowed representative on earth

The title 'Antichrist' occurs only in I Jn 2:18, 2:22 and 4:3 and II Jn 1:7; no prophetic book contains the title, which is why many commentators prefer the title 'Beast', which occurs in both the OT and NT. John tells us that there are many Antichrists but one is to come, although his spirit is already active. This significant latter day one cannot be revealed until after the Rapture. To qualify for a title which means false Messiah or false Christ, he will have to be a king – the Little Horn of Daniel chapter 7:21-24 among ten other kings; the Wilful King of Dan 11:36; the covenant maker and breaker of Dan 9:27; the one of whom Jesus said: *"if another shall come in his own name, him ye will receive"* (Jn 5:43); the blasphemous throne usurper of II Thess 2 4 and the one to whom the False Prophet is to direct worship. The False Prophet, who is said to come from the Land, rather than being expressly said to be Jewish (Rev 13:11) might well prove to be at least half Jewish and half Islamic, in order to be accepted by the Orthodox hierarchy, and to support the Beast's negotiation for the rebuilt Temple. But I must emphasise that we have no direct confirmation.

7.4. MYSTERY BABYLON
'Mystery' is not part of the title, although it appears to be in some English translations; it is descriptive. Also it instructs us to be cautious. This and the following two sections need to be

understood together to give a basic understanding of events which I have covered in greater depth in other books. Post-Diluvian history is about to run full-circle. As we have already seen, after the Flood Satanic sponsored religious rebellion against God began at Babel on the Plain of Shinar. And it is specifically the Plain of Shinar, the destination of Wickedness returning from repenting Israel in the vision of Zech 5:5-11, where it will finally be discarded by its architect. It will have outlived its purpose, having brought Satan to the point of virtual global worship among the unsaved. It is on the same Plain that the feet and toes of Nebuchadnezzar's prophetic image first appeared and where they will be struck, when the God of Heaven sets up a kingdom which will never be destroyed (Dan 2:35,44) – incidentally that kingdom emphatically does NOT conform to the Church as has been suggested. But for around three and a half years Mystery Babylon will prove to be the hideous melting pot of all false religion – the ultimate harlot faith. As the woman she is the city: *"the woman which thou sawest is that great city, which reigneth over the kings of the earth"* (Rev 17:18); as the harlot she is the multi-faceted religious monster *"With whom the kings of the earth have committed fornication, and the inhabitants of the earth have been made drunk with the wine of her fornication"* (Rev 17:2). One cannot help but feel that the present behaviour on the world scene of the Islamic Jihadist is like one intoxicated by some spiritual power, rather than by mere dedication or even fanaticism.

Although the Beast's own empire is to be Roman in ancestry, the mention of the seven-hilled city, reminiscent of Rome, and the Mesopotamian Babylon suggest a major input from both apostate Christianity and Islam; jointly they may dominate this religious harlot. We cannot be emphatic here. Adultery in worship in the Bible is when people claim to worship their God, but in fact worship another. Israel was the wife of Jehovah; the Church is the espoused Bride of Christ; within both there has often been such adultery, but in the case of Israel it finally reached the point sufficient for her, as a Wife, to have been put aside for many centuries, but never abandoned: *"Yet the number of the children of Israel shall be as the sand of the sea, which cannot be measured nor numbered; and it shall come to pass, that in the place where it was said unto them, Ye are not my people, there it shall be said unto them, Ye are the sons of the living God"* (Hos 1:10 - see also 14:4). There is not the slightest hint of any replacement wife there. However by that time the espoused Bride, the Church, will have at the Rapture been taken home to the prepared place (Jn 14:2) in the Father's House, and only the apostate dregs of Christianity will be left, perhaps with its headquarters identified in this verse: *"Here is the mind which hath wisdom. The seven heads are seven mountains, on which the woman sitteth"* (Rev17:9).

After the Rapture the 4,000 year long conflict between Isaac's seed and Ishmael's reaches its climax. It is worth recalling that **Islam was not there for the first two and half thousand years and need not be there, at least not in its present form, for the last seven!** Those seven years will culminate with the visible Return of the Lion of the Tribe of Judah, the ultimate confirmation of God's choice of the long-suffering line of Isaac and Jacob, rather than that of Ishmael.

The whole of Revelation 17 should be read, but I do not wish to enter upon a detailed study, rather I will concentrate on the demise of religious Babylon as she is to appear during the Beginning of Sorrows. At first she is introduced as being in charge of the Beast *"So he carried me away in the spirit into the wilderness: and I saw a woman sit upon a scarlet coloured beast, full of names of blasphemy, having seven heads and ten horns"* (Rev 17:3). This is the First Beast of Rev 13:1, whose worship is to be orchestrated by the Second Beast or False Prophet: *"I…… saw a beast rise up out of the sea, having seven heads and ten horns, and upon his horns ten crowns, and upon his heads the name of blasphemy…..and the dragon gave him his power, and his seat, and great authority"* (Rev 13:1-2).

The end-time significance of these ten kings is evidently to be taken particularly seriously, because they conform, with different emphases in each instance, to the ten toes of Nebuchadnezzar's visionary image of Daniel 2, to the ten horns of Daniel's vision in his Chapter 7 and to the (First) Beast of Rev 13:1. In Daniel 2 the ten toes are the concluding feature of the great image in Nebuchadnezzar's dream, the interpretation of which God gave through Daniel. Nebuchadnezzar saw the four great empires which, during the Times of the Gentiles, were only at the early stage of their successive reigns. All were to include the Holy Land and Jerusalem within their territory.

The first empire was, of course, Babylon, represented by the head of gold. The upper torso of silver was Medo-Persia and the lower torso and thighs Greece; these three empires were actually named. The legs were of iron, representing Rome, a name unfamiliar in Babylon at the time of the vision, and the feet and toes were of incompatible iron and ceramic (not 'miry' as in AV) clay. The Church Age was unknown to Nebuchadnezzar and Daniel, so it may be argued that it fits into a long unobserved gap between the legs and feet – after all, this was a dream, not a feat of engineering! It is a question of whether the legs are intended to span the Church Age or not; personally I don't think they do, because, a third of the way through the present age a new unannounced empire, the Islamic Ottoman, encompassed the Holy Land and its residue still tramples the Temple site underfoot.

A much debated but undecided question is whether in the End Times the feet and legs represent a Revived nominally Christian Roman Empire or the Islamic power, or indeed, an alliance or unnatural merger of the two. When one looks at a map of the old Roman Empire, based around the entire Mediterranean Sea with odd extensions here and there, one may observe that it is currently dominated by two groups of nations - Islamic states and nations long considered to be Christian. The ten kings subordinate to the Beast in an unnatural iron and clay confederacy could conceivably come from both camps. However strongly we feel, we should remember that there is still mystery here. Even the ancestry of the Beasts is unclear. Students of prophecy still have some legitimate scope to disagree about the details

One interpretation of Daniel chapter 7 suggests that the Beast's empire may eventually encompass the territory of all four previous empires, from Hadrian's or the Antonine Wall to the Indus, from the Atlas Mountains to the Karakoram. These are fascinating studies, but we must press on. In fact the extent of the Beast's domain seems to vary during the Tribulation Period. It will probably take a little time for him to establish his power base, deal with three challengers (Dan 7:8) and achieve worldwide adulation; although he will have powerful support. But such will be the ever increasing horrors, deprivation, starvation and general suffering even in the Beginning of Sorrows, and especially during the Great Tribulation, together with the Beast's own tyrannical misrule, that throughout the world armies and marauding parties with a variety of loyalties will probably be constantly on the move, even if only those affecting the Holy Land are actually recorded in Bible prophecy.

There is no need to discuss Babylon the Great of Revelation chapter 18, as it is the depraved political, commercial, social and even entertainment aspect of the same end-time monstrosity, devoid of all moral restraint and the home of fraud, corruption, murder and every imaginable vice. It is to survive the rather earlier demise of its religious element until its spectacular overthrow at the end of the Great Tribulation (Rev 18:2,21). However I see no particular reason to connect Babylon the Great more with Islam than with any other culture or religion, unless possibly regarding the Plain of Shinar location of Babylon.

7.5. TEN KINGS WHICH DESTROY BABYLONIAN RELIGION
We note in Rev 17 that these kings start their brief reign to some

extent supported by the influential harlot, but that, as soon as they are able, they turn on the harlot, whom they actually hate, and destroy her. This is the end of the ancient religion which started with Nimrod, and has culminated with this abominable multi-faith monstrosity: *"And the ten horns which thou sawest are ten kings, which have received no kingdom as yet; but receive power as kings one hour with the beast. These have one mind, and shall give their power and strength unto the beast. These shall make war with the Lamb, and the Lamb shall overcome them: for he is Lord of lords, and King of kings….. And the ten horns which thou sawest upon the beast, these shall hate the whore, and shall make her desolate and naked, and shall eat her flesh, and burn her with fire. For **God hath put in their hearts to fulfil his will**, and to agree, and give their kingdom unto the beast, until the words of God shall be fulfilled"* (Rev 17:12-14,16-17). God is using Satan's closest emissary to destroy the monster which Satan has been nurturing since the Flood. Whether anything remains thereafter of either apostate Christianity or Islam as religions is doubtful. Like many other commentators, I can be no more precise than that. By giving their open allegiance to the Satanic Beast, these kings are automatically confronting Christ Himself, in His role as the Lamb, who had inaugurated the Tribulation Period (Rev 5:6): *"These have one mind, and shall give their power and strength unto the beast. These shall make war with the Lamb, and the Lamb shall overcome them: for he is Lord of lords, and King of kings: and they that are with him are called, and chosen, and faithful"* (Rev 17:13-14).

During the Great Tribulation, all who will have rejected the preaching of the Gospel of the Kingdom will be spiritually intoxicated, no longer by the discarded Babylonian harlot, but by the mesmeric power of the Trinity of Evil: *"And they worshipped the dragon which gave power unto the beast: and they worshipped the beast, saying, Who is like unto the beast? who is able to make war with him? And there was given unto him a mouth speaking great things and blasphemies; and power was given unto him to continue forty and two months"* (Rev 13:4-5).

7.6. THE TRIBULATION TEMPLE

The idea of a future Jewish Temple on the Temple Mount, between the Al Aqsa Mosque and Dome on the Rock would at present be anathema to all Muslims. We have no guarantee that either of these buildings will be left standing following the Rapture; but they might well be, as none of the end-time earthquakes *appears* to be quite so early. It may be that the Beast, with Satan's support will be able cynically to negotiate some sort of arrangement with Islamic leaders, leaving a trio of temples. We cannot be sure. The later Millennial Temple of Ezekiel will have no such pagan neighbours; the area having almost certainly been cleared by the earthquake of Zech 14:4. In fact the whole geology of the area will be massively changed by that earthquake, which is to split the Mount of Olives east and west, forming a great valley, which must surely split the Temple Mount, and cause a great uplift on the northern side. Prophecies from Isa 2:2-3, Mic 4:1-2 and much of Ezekiel chapters 40 to 48 apply. I have devoted much of chapter 7 of *"The Millennium – Restoration After Retribution"* to this topic.

At 7.1. I promised to say more about the seven year duration of the Tribulation Period. We have to turn to a very clear prophecy, with a vitally important future application confirmed by the Lord Jesus Christ Himself in His Olivet Discourse, **the seven year period immediately prior to Christ's Return in Power has been declared to be specifically for the Jews** – or Daniel's people. Muslims and so called Christian Replacement Theologians inevitably resent this inconvenient truth; Muslims have the better excuse as it is not in the Koran. It is Gabriel (Dan 9:21) who is entrusted to reveal the equal lengths of the two contrasting parts of the Tribulation Period. Here I am adapting a section from *"God's Timetable for a Troubled World"*, which I made succinct at the time and am now further condensing!

Gabriel told Daniel, *"Seventy weeks are determined upon **thy people and upon thy holy city**, to finish the transgression, and to make an end of sins, and to make reconciliation for iniquity, and to bring in everlasting righteousness, and to seal up the vision and prophecy, and to anoint the most Holy. Know therefore and understand, that from the going forth of the commandment to restore and to build Jerusalem unto Messiah the Prince shall be seven weeks, and threescore and two weeks: the street shall be built again, and the wall, even in troublous times. And after threescore and two weeks shall Messiah be cut off, but not for himself:* and *the people"* (the Romans) *"of the prince that shall come"* (the Beast) *shall destroy the city and the sanctuary"* (Rome in 70 AD); *"and the end thereof shall be with a flood, and unto the end of the war desolations are determined. And **he"** **(the Beast) "shall confirm the covenant with many for one week** (seven years): and in the midst of the week* (at the 3½ year point) **he shall cause the sacrifice and the oblation to cease, and for the overspreading of abominations he shall make it desolate**, *even until the consummation, and that determined shall be poured upon the desolate"* (Dan 9:24-27). This will be a temple unblessed by God, a joint enterprise between the Beast for his own sinister purposes and Orthodox Jewish priests for theirs. We find confirmation that this is to be a Jerusalem Temple in Matt 24:15 and Mk 13:14, where Gospel readers are commanded to understand! Have you taken the trouble?

The entire Church Age lies between the sixty-ninth and seventieth week of years. The above Daniel 9 passage is generally considered as the main authority for a Revived Roman Empire. However we should not be over-hasty in defining the exact constitution of this Revived Roman Empire; the current volatility of both the European Union and the Mediterranean Islamic states is something which the Beast **may** be the first to bring to a peaceful settlement, or use as a basis for a united empire - for his own ends of course. Anybody who can achieve that would be hailed as a world-class leader.

The Demise of Ancient Religions and Feuding Nations

The word translated 'week' can mean any heptad or group of seven. 490 lunar (360 day) years or 70 septennia were said to be allocated to (literally set aside for) Daniel's people, starting with a precisely identified day in 445 BC. This is about Jews, not the Gentile Church. We may forget here the first division after 49 years, though it was very important within Old Testament history. We are thus left with two groups of 69 sevens or 483 elapsed years plus 7 future years. The 483 elapsed years take us to what we call the first Palm Sunday, when Jesus as Messiah the Prince entered His city to be *"cut off"*. Seven years are thus left in abeyance for Daniel's people until after the Rapture of the Church. Written simply, it amounts to:

7 + 62 + 1 = 70 groups of seven years or 49 + 434 + 7 = 490 years

So, as soon as possible after the Rapture, the false prince, Antichrist or Beast is going either to negotiate or to impose this seven year covenant with Israel. We may ask why he should do this if Satan hates Israel so much. We do know from this chapter of Daniel and from II Thess 2:4 and Rev 11:1-2 that there must be such a future rebuilt Temple, with sacrifices and offerings resumed at last after more than nineteen centuries, and that after three and a half years the Beast will break his cynical covenant, put a stop to these ordinances and usurp the throne, the Mercy Seat of, one assumes, a replacement Ark of the Covenant. We must remember that Jerusalem is the place of God's earthly throne to which Satan will aspire, having been cast out of the Heavens (Rev 12:9 etc), and that Babylon is the ancient place of Satan's earthly throne, though after the sack of Babylon it was for many centuries transferred to Pergamos (Rev 2:12-13), with some of its titles later moved to Rome.

During the Tribulation period God will have been sending out His evangelists – 144,000 sealed Jews, saved following the Rapture and mightily empowered by His Holy Spirit. to the entire world to preach the Gospel of the Kingdom. David Baron writes:

    As among the Pharisees in the days of Christ, so among

the Talmudical Jews, there are many 'Nathaniels' of whom it may be said that they are 'according to the law, blameless' – men walking consistently according to the light they have, and whose lives are a noble example of religious zeal".
They evidently will not be saved in time to be taken at the Rapture; but God has reserved them for a very special mission. *"And this gospel of the kingdom shall be preached in all the world for a witness unto all nations; and then shall the end come:* (Matt 24:14); *"Hurt not the earth, neither the sea, nor the trees, till we have sealed the servants of our God in their foreheads. And I heard the number of them which were sealed: and there were sealed an hundred and forty and four thousand of all the tribes of the children of Israel"* (Rev 7:3-4); they are the evangelists and these are their converts: *"And one of the elders answered, saying unto me, What are these which are arrayed in white robes? and whence came they? And I said unto him, Sir, thou knowest. And he said to me, These are they which came out of great tribulation, and have washed their robes, and made them white in the blood of the Lamb"* (Rev 7:13-14). It seems that following the Rapture there will be a 'Second Pentecost', the Joel 2:16-17 prophecy having been only partially fulfilled at the first one. Also one might say that there will be a second Emmaus: *"Then opened he their understanding, that they might understand the scriptures"* (Lk 24:45). Like the two on the Emmaus road, they had been blind to Messianic prophecy; now they will preach it!

The coverage of these evangelists will be global, because God has so commissioned them, and we may be sure that they will preach Christ crucified as widely in Muslims lands as anywhere else, something long impossible. But from what we have seen in these four sections, we can fairly safely conclude that by the mid-point of the Tribulation Period, all false religion will have given way to the overt worship of Satan through his appointed stooge, the Beast. The relevant closing verses of Revelation 13 have already been quoted. **Islam as a religion will probably be no more.**

7.7. A SUICIDAL NORTHERN JIHAD?

The Shi-ite Hadith corruption – and it clearly is a corruption - of Ezekiel chapters 38 and 39 is fascinating, because it has so many parallels to the Bible original. Because it is nearer the Bible original than so much else in Islamic teaching, the authors of the Hadith versions could well be aware of its latter day importance, as well as the embarrassing (for them) outcome for Islamic nations of the Ezekiel original. We must devote some space here, not to do a complete analysis of the Bible account, but to summarise it in sufficient depth to illustrate the promised fate of the Islamic participants. Asking a Muslim, particularly a Shi-ite, to read the Bible version could be a helpful move, although probably not a good opening gambit. In the Hadiths an 'amutual alliance' - armies from the north, including that of what they currently regard as a recently Christian nation (Russia), are to descend upon Israel at the time of the destruction of the Dajjal (Antichrist) by A'isa, Son of Miriam; but thereafter the armies, as in the Bible, will turn upon each other. Allah, they say, will destroy the enemies in a single night.

Ezekiel chapter 39 is largely an elaboration of chapter 38, so we can concentrate on 38, though both chapters should be read in full. We can leave the identity of Gog and the difficult question of timing for a page or so; the following verses give some general pointers:-

- *"Thus saith the Lord GOD; Behold, I am against thee, O Gog, the chief prince of Meshech and Tubal"* (38:3). It is God Himself who confronts the leader of the invasion.
- *"Persia, Ethiopia, and Libya with them; all of them with shield and helmet: Gomer, and all his bands; the house of Togarmah of the north quarters, and all his bands* (38:6). As far as they can reasonably be identified, these are currently all Islamic nations. The invasion is described as factual, not visionary; historians agree that no such invasion has taken place as yet, so it can only be future.

- *"In the latter years thou shalt come into the land that is brought back from the sword, and is gathered out of many people, against the mountains of Israel, which have been always waste: but it is brought forth out of the nations, and they shall dwell safely all of them"* (38:8). This suggests, rather than affirms, that it is to take place during the very brief interval within the Tribulation period between the end or partial end of the *Diaspora* and that of the Times of the Gentiles.
- *"And thou shalt come from thy place out of the north parts, thou, and many people with thee, all of them riding upon horses, a great company, and a mighty army: And thou shalt come up against **my people of Israel**, as a cloud to cover the land; it shall be in the latter days, and I will bring thee against **my land**, that the heathen may know me, when I shall be sanctified in thee, O Gog, before their eyes"* (Ezek 38:15-16). It is Gog who is addressed by God as coming from the north. It is to be a quite massive invasion, described in terms that had to be understood for around 2,500 years before tanks, guided missiles and other complex military hardware. God's victory will be recognised among the heathens as news of the event and its outcome spreads, no doubt helping to enhance the preaching throughout the world of the 144,000.
- *"In my jealousy and in the fire of my wrath have I spoken, Surely in that day there shall be a great shaking in the land of Israel"* (38:19). Here is a reminder of how God's wrath will be evident in that day. During the Beginning of Sorrows there will still be unbelievers in Israel to be shaken.
- *"And I will call for a sword against him throughout all my mountains, saith the Lord GOD: **every man's sword shall be against his brother**"* (38:21). God has done this before, as with the Midianites in Gideon's day. There is nothing in the text to say that the mutual slaughter is between Shia and Sunni; on the other hand there is

nothing to say that it is not; and these are much the best known divisions within Islam. This appears to be a major stage in the discrediting and demise of Islamic influence. It could cause millions of Muslims to question their own faith.

- *"And I will plead against him with pestilence and with blood; and I will rain upon him, and upon his bands, and upon the many people that are with him, an overflowing rain, and great hailstones, fire, and brimstone"* (38:22). In addition to the mutual slaughter, there will be disease and other terrifying phenomena.

- *"And I will magnify myself, and sanctify myself, and I will be known in the eyes of many nations, and **they shall know that I am Jehovah"*** (38:23 Dby). This seems to indicate that the invasion will take place before the Great Tribulation starts at the mid-point of the seven years, when recognition of the acts of the true God will be less hazardous than later. After that the worship of the Beast and acceptance of his 666 Mark (Rev 14:9) will put millions beyond possible redemption. The world shall be left in no doubt that this defeat upon the mountains of Israel is the hand Jehovah, rather than of Allah as in the Hadiths.

Another reason for thinking that the invasion is likely to occur during the Beginning of Sorrows, is because, (a) it is very different in national identities and in final outcome from the later wars of the Great Tribulation, and (b) because the invader declares: *"And thou shalt say, I will go up to the land of unwalled villages; I will go to them that are at rest, that dwell safely, all of them dwelling without walls, and having neither bars nor gates"* (Ezekiel 38:11). Any militarily undefended Israel before the Rapture, and indeed before the seven year treaty with the coming Beast-emperor, seems highly improbable.

The statement in 39:2 in the AV/KJV, *"I will turn thee back, and leave but the sixth part of thee"* is a mistranslation of a difficult sentence; evidently none will return home. The rest of that verse is correct: *"and will cause thee to come up from the north parts, and will bring thee upon the mountains of Israel."* That is where God will judge them, and at verse 39:11 we learn that the bodies will, over a period of seven months, be buried beyond Jordan. From this one can make a case for it being at least seven months before the mid-point. Certainly it proves that this cannot be the same event as Armageddon. Ezekiel 39:21-29 tells how this is all leading up to the ultimate salvation of Israel; but that is outside our terms of reference. This invasion is led by Gog, and not Gog **and** Magog as in the event described in Rev 20:8 following the Millennium; the two differ in many respects, but are still sometimes confused.

Scholars have long debated the identities of Gog and his allies. One thing is clear; these are not the nearer neighbours of Israel as described in Psalm 83 and Daniel 11, which we will consider in the next sections. They are from further afield. Here I adapt a paragraph from *'God's Timetable for a Troubled World'*.

Oddly enough the identity of *the "Gog of the land of Magog"*, the prime mover in this invasion, is more doubtful than his allies..... Verse 38:15 says that Gog will be from the far North, and Moscow is almost due north of Jerusalem and very distant, and certainly Russia is currently Iran's most loyal ally. However there are instances in the OT where eastern nations approaching Israel via the usual Fertile Crescent route are said to be from the north, the direction of their crossing the national border. As far back as the 4th Century B.C., rabbis identified Gog as coming from the area of Afghanistan and Pakistan; thus the former Soviet Islamic nations of Central Asia could well be included. Persia is of course Iran; Ethiopia refers more to the Sudan than the former Abyssinia, and Libya is simply Libya; Meschech and Tubal were identified in Genesis as sons of Japheth, rather than Shem, and the cities named after them are found elsewhere in the OT, ruling out the common association with Moscow and Tobol'sk. Togarmah and Gomer are also

The Demise of Ancient Religions and Feuding Nations

descended from Japheth, so are much more likely to be Scythian, from the steppes around and beyond the Caspian Sea, than from Turkey, as has been suggested.

So can this be described as a jihad or Islamic holy war? It could be, in view of the fact that most participating nations will be or will have been Islamic; but it could also be an opportunist political resource and land-grabbing attack by rivals on the Beast's Empire, which will probably at that stage not yet be worldwide. This would explain the absence from the alliance of closer neighbours of Israel, who will almost certainly be from within the territory of the Beast's empire.

Our Lord told us: *"For nation shall rise against nation, and kingdom against kingdom: and there shall be famines, and pestilences, and earthquakes, in divers places. All these are the beginning of sorrows"* (Matt 24:7-8). The effects of the opening in Heaven of the earlier Seals (Rev 6:1 et seq) will have been sorely felt, provoking invasions of nations thought to be materially better off. The political map of the world will certainly be considerably changed by the end of the invasion. Further evidence that this invasion will take place during the first half of the Tribulation Period, rather than later, is the fact that Jesus, in Matt 24:15-20, warned Jewish believers, those who will heed His words, that when they see the Abomination of Desolation set up in the Temple they should flee to the desert or wilderness. This invasion therefore seems to be well before the Abomination. While it is not actually stated in Ezekiel's prophecy, it does seem more likely that God will intervene against the invasion when more of His people are still there to be saved from calamity. The battle for Jerusalem at the end of the Great Tribulation, which we consider at 7.10., will be different in several respects.

7.8. WARS OF THE GREAT TRIBULATION

Now while we know from various Old Testament prophecies, from the Olivet Discourse and from Revelation, that war will characterise the Great Tribulation, no other end-time war is described in anything like the detail of the Ezekiel 38 and 39 one which we have just reviewed, in which God has said He will be recognised and glorified. Correlating the descriptions of other battles is difficult, and we must bear in mind that our main interest is to see how the Ishmael and Isaac conflict will feature in the days leading up to Armageddon, rather than covering the world scene.

Isaiah chapters 14 to 23 prophesy coming judgment upon Babylon, Philistia, Moab, Syria, Ethiopia, Egypt, Elam and Tyre, with only Egypt of this group being told of ultimate blessing. But the difficulty is that, without going through these prophecies in great detail, it is not always easy to distinguish between different phases of judgments, and even what referred to the past, what to the End Times and what to both; there are various similar prophecies in other OT books, which we have not taken time to look at, which present the same difficulties. The passages which we are quoting in this chapter should be sufficient to demonstrate that what are currently Islamic nations feature prominently.

In Daniel chapter 11 we encounter a further Middle East war, where all the nations involved are currently Islamic. Bearing in mind that the first four verses of Daniel 12 are better included in chapter 11, the Great Tribulation timing is definite. *"And at that time shall Michael stand up, the great prince which standeth for the children of thy people: and there shall be a time of trouble, such as never was since there was a nation even to that same time: and at that time thy people shall be delivered, every one that shall be found written in the book"* (Dan 12:1). It is the time which Jesus spoke of in Matt 24:21-22 already quoted. However it will neither be the final siege of Jerusalem nor the Battle of Armageddon, which we cover in 7.10. It must therefore be a little earlier.

Prominent is the Wilful King, whose description confirms that he is indeed the Beast: *"And the king shall do according to his will; and he shall exalt himself, and magnify himself above every*

The Demise of Ancient Religions and Feuding Nations

*god, and shall speak marvellous things against the God of gods; and he shall prosper till the indignation be accomplished; for that which is determined shall be done. Neither shall he regard the **gods of his fathers**, nor the desire of women, nor regard any god; for he shall magnify himself above all"* (Dan 11:36-37 ASV). The words *'God of his fathers'* in the AV and NKJV is wrong; *elohim,* which appears in these verses, in some contexts can be translated as God, but more often, as here, it means gods. The earlier part of that chapter of Daniel gives such an accurate prophetic account of events of the Inter-Testament or Apocryphal era, where various end-time personalities are foreshadowed and their ancestry explained, that, after eight hundred years of acceptance of the genuineness of the prophecy, an atheist historian-philosopher called Porphyry claimed that this was a fraudulent document dating from around 175 BC; in modern times agnostic liberal theologians in various seminaries love any such lie which denies the Divine inspiration of the Bible. The lightning speed rise and expansion of Alexander the Great's empire took place during the 4th Century BC. Following his death, his empire was divided into four, and during the next couple of centuries until the Roman conquests reached it, the Holy Land lay between the territories of the rival Seleucid Greek kingdom, with its capital at Antioch and the Ptolemaic Greek kingdom in Egypt, whose last monarch was Cleopatra. Thus we had the prototypes of the King of the North and King of the South; some of their activities and the courageous Jewish resistance are covered in the Apocrypha, having been partially foretold in Zechariah as well as Daniel. Then in verses 32 to 35 we have what many commentators consider to be a general commentary on the intervening twenty one plus centuries. The sudden switch without warning from pre-First Coming to near-Second Coming prophecy is quite common in the Old Testament.

Whilst the Beast is based at Jerusalem – though we don't not know whether he will remain there following his Temple desecration or simply leave his Abomination as a sign of his presence - we find the King of the South attacking the King of the North and throwing his weight around in Israel in the process: *"And at the time of the end shall the king of the south push at him: and the king of the north shall come against him like a whirlwind, with chariots, and with horsemen, and with many ships; and he shall enter into the countries, and shall overflow and pass over. He shall enter also into the glorious land, and many countries shall be overthrown: but these shall escape out of his hand, even Edom, and Moab, and the chief of the children of Ammon"* (11:40-41).

The three little states east of the Jordan, now part of the kingdom of that name, were not Roman imperial territory and are to be left intact to feature a little later. Perhaps this will be because the desert refuge, to which believers in Judea will be urged to flee when the Abomination of Desolation begins to appear in Jerusalem, will be there; part of the area is still desert. *"And the woman"* (Israel from the context) *"fled into the wilderness, where she hath a place prepared of God, that they should feed her there a thousand two hundred and threescore days"* (Rev 12:6) in fulfilment of Matt 24:16-20 and Mk 13:14-18. This explains the otherwise enigmatic prophecy in Isa 63:1: *"Who is this that cometh from Edom, with dyed garments from Bozrah? this that is glorious in his apparel, travelling in the greatness of his strength? I that speak in righteousness, mighty to save"*. Hab 3:3, which should be interpreted in the future tense, supports this: *"God came from Teman, and the Holy One from mount Paran. His glory covered the heavens, and the earth was full of his praise."* Immediately after His Return in Power, the Lord, *mighty to save*, is to attend to these, his obedient refugees. There, in the very heart of what has for all these centuries been Islamic territory, God purposes to set up a Jewish refuge for the three and a half years of the Great Tribulation. How wonderful!

Some feel that the King of the North is the Beast; the pronouns in this part of Daniel are rather ambiguous – we would know for certain if we needed to, as Tribulation saints will. Some feel that his domain will be a revived Assyria. While Old Testament prophecy makes it clear that the ancient Assyrian capital of Nineveh will rise no more (Nahum 1:14), it is equally clear that Assyria will again be a nation, continuing into the Millennium along with Egypt (Isa 19:23-24). Already there is within the 'Assyrian Triangle', bordering Kurdistan, and mainly in northern Iraq, but spilling over into Turkey, Iran and Syria, a distinct Assyrian ethnic group calling for independence. They once had a sizeable Christian minority which was slaughtered by the Ottomans at the same time as the Armenians in 1915. There are verses in Micah and particularly Nahum which talk of a latter day Assyria. While there have been Christian and other minorities, all these, less the aforementioned Moab, Edom and Ammon, are nations where Islam has long been dominant; but they are not specifically Ishmaelite nations, which God appears to have reserved for even later judgment.

7.9. ISRAEL'S NEARER NEIGHBOURS

There is a passage in Psalm 83 which many commentators do not see as having any end-time significance. Admittedly it is described as a confederacy rather than an actual invasion; but the intention is clearly aggressive. And, as Bishop Perowne and Professor AF Kirkpatrick point out, there has never in the past been an alliance such as is described here, so a future invasion must be considered: *"They have said, Come, and let us cut them off from being a nation; that the name of Israel may be no more in remembrance. For they have consulted together with one consent: they are confederate against thee: The tabernacles of Edom, and the Ishmaelites; of Moab, and the Hagarenes; Gebal, and Ammon, and Amalek; the Philistines with the inhabitants of Tyre; Assur also is joined with them: they have holpen the children of Lot"* (Ps 83:4-8). We quoted part of this passage at 4.10. Three of these we dealt with in the previous section. Asshur is of course Assyria. Most of the peoples listed are descendants of Abraham, but none by Sarah and the child of promise. Assyria is descended from Abraham's brother, Nahor. The unrelated Philistines and Tyre were at least very near neighbours. JN Darby, commenting on this Psalm, writes:

> "In Psalm 83 it is the way that man is guilty of active enmity against God, in his hatred against God's people, using craft, conspiracy and violence to destroy their remembrance off the earth, the result being that Jehovah alone (the God of Israel) is the most high over all the earth; for such is the effect of man's efforts."

Islam has not been alone in hating God's ancient people, but for over fourteen centuries it has been foremost; so much against Jehovah's people has been done in the name of Allah. Those who claim that these are one and the same are either ignorant of Holy Scripture or choose deliberately to ignore the evidence.

We simply cannot quote all the numerous prophecies which have at least some end-time relevance concerning these ancient bitter enemies of Israel; we looked at some in 4.9. Some of these nations which disappeared thousands of years ago are to reappear in the Tribulation Period, only to be destroyed for ever: *"Though I make a full end of all nations whither I have scattered thee, yet will I not make a full end of thee: but I will correct thee in measure, and will not leave thee altogether unpunished"* (Jer 30:11); *"The indignation of the Lord is against all nations, and His fury against all their armies….. For the Lord has a great sacrifice in Bozrah, and a great slaughter in the land of Edom….. For it is the day of the Lord's vengeance, the year of recompense for Zion"* (Isa 34:2,6,8). See also Isa 63:1-7, where we read of Jehovah's treading the winepress alone and tramping them in His fury. *"I shall see him, but not now: I shall behold him, but not nigh: there shall come a Star out of Jacob, and a Sceptre shall rise out of Israel, and shall smite the corners of Moab, and destroy all the children of Sheth"* (Numb 24:17). *"Because thou hast said, These two nations and these two countries shall be mine, and we will possess it; whereas the LORD was there….. Thus saith the Lord GOD; When the whole earth rejoiceth, I will make thee desolate. As thou didst rejoice at the inheritance of the house of Israel, because it was desolate, so will I do unto thee: thou shalt be desolate, O mount Seir, and all Idumea, even all of it: and they shall know that I am the LORD"* (Ezek 35:10-15). God's memory is longer than some care to believe.

7.10. ARMAGEDDON – THE JERUSALEM BATTLE FRONT

During the Great Tribulation there will be a thorough sifting and refining of Israel to the point where only one third will come through the test: *"And I will bring the third part into the fire, and will refine them as silver is refined, and will try them as gold is tried. They shall call on my name, and I will answer them: I will say, It is my people; and they shall say, Jehovah"* (His covenant Name) *"is my God"* (Zech 13:9 Dby). See also Isa 4:3-4, Ezek 22:21-22 and Amos 9:9.

The terms of reference of this book confine us mainly at this stage to prophecy concerning Israel and what is to be left of Islam in the final phase of the Great Tribulation. In the following three verses we again see God introducing Himself by His covenant name, Jehovah, which is why I continue to quote the Darby version when appropriate. His burden here is for Israel. He draws our attention to the *"people round about"* or *"surrounding nations"* (NKJV) before turning to *"all the nations of the earth"*. The surrounding nations which will get there most easily are to be first to feel His wrath. *"The burden of the word of Jehovah concerning Israel. Thus saith Jehovah, who stretcheth out the heavens, and layeth the foundation of the earth, and formeth the spirit of man within him: Behold, I will make Jerusalem a cup of bewilderment unto all the peoples round about, and also against Judah shall it be in the siege against Jerusalem. And it shall come to pass in that day that I will make Jerusalem a burdensome stone unto all peoples: all that burden themselves with it shall certainly be wounded, and all the nations of the earth shall be assembled together against it"* (Zech 12:1-3 Dby); *"For my sword is bathed in the heavens; behold, it shall come down upon Edom, and upon the people of my ban, to judgment….. For it is the day of Jehovah's vengeance, the year of recompenses for the controversy of Zion"* (Isa 34:5,8 Dby).

"Nations of the earth" cannot mean 'people of the (Holy) Land', because those whom we saw in the last section, with the exception of the Philistines, are not actually of the Land, and, even more importantly, the book of Revelation makes it clear that the whole world will be represented in the forces which are to assemble at the end of the Great Tribulation to make war with the coming Christ (16:14,16; 19:19); furthermore, the Euphrates would not have to be dried up to facilitate the passage of the Kings of East, were these to be local. Rev 9:16 tells of a coming army of two hundred million; the Middle East cannot provide such numbers!

However the more distant armies are likely to take weeks at least, more likely months, to assemble, in a world where the various Trumpet and Bowl of Wrath judgments will probably have paralysed electronic guidance systems and much other military hardware. The nearer forces, all from currently Islamic lands, are evidently first going to be humbled by God, but in a way contrasting with Armageddon, where, following the fate of the Beast and False Prophet, we are told: *"And the remnant were slain with the sword of him that sat upon the horse, which sword proceeded out of his mouth"* (Rev 19:21).

God has said: *"In that day will I make the leaders of Judah like a hearth of fire among wood, and like a torch of fire in a sheaf; and they shall devour all the peoples round about, on the right hand and on the left; and Jerusalem shall dwell again in her own place, in Jerusalem..... In that day will Jehovah defend the inhabitants of Jerusalem; and he that stumbleth among them at that day shall be as David; and the house of David as God, as the Angel of Jehovah before them. And it shall come to pass in that day, that I will seek to destroy all the nations that come against Jerusalem. And I will pour upon the house of David and upon the inhabitants of Jerusalem the spirit of grace and of supplications; and they shall look on me whom they pierced, and they shall mourn for him, as one mourneth for an only son, and shall be in bitterness for him, as one that is in bitterness for his firstborn"* (Zech 12:6,8-10 Dby). Either we believe the Bible or we don't; few things could be clearer.

As we were reminded in the first chapter, back in Elijah's time, unbeknown to the prophet, God had reserved for Himself seven thousand who had not bowed the knee to Baal (I Kings 19:18). So, during the Great Tribulation, He is going to reserve in or around Jerusalem a band of faithful Jews who will not bow the knee to the Beast. Two wonderful things are to happen. Firstly, God is going to empower mightily these survivors of Judah and Jerusalem to destroy their ancient enemies, as He empowered the Children of Israel with miraculous victories back in the time of Joshua. Secondly, there will be great mourning mixed with mighty wonder, as they look upon the One whom their forbears pierced, when dramatically Christ's great 'until' is fulfilled: *"For I say unto you, Ye shall not see me henceforth,* ***till ye shall say****, Blessed is he that cometh in the name of the Lord"* (Matt 23:39). The remainder of Zechariah 12 describes this national heartfelt mourning. Only then will take place the national rebirth prophesied in Isa 66:8-9 quoted back at 5.9.

7.11. AN ISLAMIC ANTICHRIST?
I first encountered the idea of an Islamic Antichrist in 1958 in Geoffrey King's commentary on Daniel, whilst stationed in the Persian Gulf, and since then, because the idea had a certain appeal, I have made a habit of looking out for evidence from Scripture. But I have always found much more against the concept than for it, though in most other respects I found Geoffrey's book to be very helpful. I met him a few years later. He writes: "You keep your eye today upon what is called 'The Moslem Belt,' from Morocco right across to India'." Well, I cannot disagree with that, but it does not disprove the more commonly held view that the Beast will arise from within what is often, as we have seen, referred to as the 'Revived Roman Empire'. The Islamic idea is more common among Post-Tribulationists. I want to be as brief as possible, and will not enlarge unnecessarily on points covered earlier in this book.

Post-Tribulation is an aberration of Pre-Millennialism. It does not expect the Rapture to take place until the end of the Great Tribulation, which would allow the Tribulation Period to creep up gradually, rather than with the clear start signal of a vanishing Church. It does not take into account that the seven year Tribulation is the detached portion of 490 years, as stated in Dan 9:24 to be **specifically** for Daniel's people, Israel (see section 7.6), unlike the intervening predominantly Gentile Church Age, which will by then be over. Post-Tribulation runs completely counter to the New Testament wedding custom teaching, where the Espoused Bride is first taken to the Bridegroom's Father's House, and only after the Marriage does the Bridegroom return with his Bride to the Bride's home for the feast. The 'Post-Trib' programme also leaves no room for the Judgment Seat of Christ for individuals before the Marriage, when the Bride must appear in her full glory. There is no merit in the common Post-Trib 'stiff upper lip' approach to supposed courageous enduring of the Tribulation, if Christ has chosen to take His espoused Bride home first.

Jesus said: *"Every kingdom divided against itself is brought to desolation; and every city or house divided against itself shall not stand: And if Satan cast out Satan, he is divided against himself; how shall then his kingdom stand?"* (Matt 12:25-26). Islam is a divided nation, furiously warring within itself, and thus displaying the seeds of its own destruction. Those who believe in an Islamic Antichrist should compare that with what Jesus said. But Islam still has the capacity to cause untold chaos. And global chaos, alarm and despondency are the very characteristics Satan will want to abound, so that he may present his Man of Sin, his strong man, as his answer to the world's problems.

Let us summarise:-
- The idea of the Islamic Antichrist has caught on in recent years with the dramatic rise of Militant Jihadism and its ever increasing atrocities. But we have seen that the religious element of Islam is almost certainly to be

The Demise of Ancient Religions and Feuding Nations

neutralised within Mystery Babylon, which will not survive the first three and a half years, whereas the Beast and His False Prophet are to survive until Armageddon.

- In the vision of Daniel 2, summarising the empires which were to occupy the Holy Land before Christ's Return to set up the Millennial (Stone) Kingdom (v 44), only four empires are listed (vv 37-40). There is no fifth available to interpret as being Islamic. The Roman iron continues from the ancient legs to the latter day feet and toes, even when ceramic clay is introduced. Unlike the earlier gold, silver and bronze, the iron is never said to be replaced.
- The Beast, as we have seen from Dan 9:26, is to be from the people who destroyed Jerusalem. When Islam took over the city in 638 AD, they did not destroy it, but rather laboured to maintain it, but as an Islamic metropolis.
- Because the legs are split within the ancient Roman Empire, one cannot reasonably claim, as has been done, that we have Sunni and Shi-ite elements represented in the feet.
- The Little Horn *"shall speak great words against the most High, and shall wear out the saints of the most High, and think to change times and laws: and they shall be given into his hand until a time and times and the dividing of time"* (Dan 7:2). This has recently been interpreted as the imposition of the Islamic calendar and Shariah Law; but there are other older interpretations. Already, without any Islamic involvement, Christian based laws are being overthrown throughout Europe, and replaced by secular, humanist laws. As this Beast has yet to be revealed, there are other ways in which he could change the seasons, such as the seven day weekly cycle imposed by God, which dates back to Creation.
- Mystery Babylon cannot be Islam, which has existed only since the 7th Century, whereas Babylon's roots go back to within two generations of the Flood, if not earlier.
- The idea of an Islamic Antichrist has been reinforced

by the recent behaviour of Islamic Fundamentalists; but Islam does not have a monopoly of cruelty and atrocities. They are being portrayed as being more evil than even the most apostate branches of Christianity. But an immensely significant factor is being overlooked. When the Church is called home, the salt of the earth will have disappeared from 'Christendom', and **there will no longer be any moral restraint** within the non-Islamic world, but rather the most incredible degradation and blasphemy. Already within 'Christendom' governments and courts have reached the stage when *"The kings of the earth set themselves, and the rulers take counsel together, against the LORD, and against his anointed, saying, Let us break their bands asunder, and cast away their cords from us"* (Ps 2:2-3). Daniel in vision sees what is to emerge from former Christendom, not Islam: *"Behold a fourth beast, dreadful and terrible, and strong exceedingly; and it had great iron teeth: it devoured and brake in pieces, and stamped the residue with the feet of it: and it was diverse from all the beasts that were before it; and it had ten horns"* (Dan 7:7).

- The Invasion of Gog and his allies is not from within the Beast's kingdom but actually trespasses within what is about to be if not already the Beast's territory.
- Were the Beast's kingdom truly to be Islamic, one would hardly expect there to be Jews living in Judea and Jerusalem to be warned to flee when the Abomination appears, and there surely would be none to defend Jerusalem against surrounding nations as in Zechariah 12.

No, the idea of an Islamic Antichrist may be a fascinating idea, with a good deal of current appeal, but the evidence of Scripture seems to make it clear that the Beast will not be Islamic. My friend, Dr Paul Wilkinson, who has travelled very widely internationally teaching end-time prophecy and related topics, and who is in close touch with most leading authorities, assures me that it is almost universally agreed among Pre-Tribulationists that, despite the current prevalence of Islamic activity, the Beast, as has long been taught by students of prophecy, will arise from within the modern variation of the Roman Empire.

CHAPTER EIGHT

The Future and Personal Options

*"How shall we escape, if we neglect so great salvation;
which at the first began to be spoken by the Lord,
and was confirmed unto us by them that heard him?"*
(Heb 2:3)

8.1. TAKING STOCK

We have delved back into the ancient origins of the conflict between Judaism and the Church on the one hand and Islam on the other. We have noted that much goes back to the lapse of faith in that man of faith, Abraham, resulting in his having a son by Hagar, and the subsequent conflict between Ishmael and Isaac. We have even taken a peep at what is to happen on earth before and after Christ's Return in Power. We have no authority to say what may yet happen **before** the Rapture, because no details are given of events in the Church Age after the fall of Jerusalem in 70 AD. But we have many admonitions in the New Testament to keep us our toes, and the signs of the times are proliferating and accelerating.

Noah spent a hundred plus years building the Ark before the Flood came, but was given only sufficient notice to collect all the animals into safety. *"By faith Noah, being warned of God of things not seen as yet, moved with fear, prepared an ark to the saving of his house; by the which he condemned the world, and became heir of the righteousness which is by faith"* (Heb 11:7). Scoffers who say that we Pre-Tribulationists are cowardly in expecting Christ to take us home before the coming disaster

The Future and Personal Options

should ponder those words. The real cowardice lies in being shy to believe or to be like Noah, *a preacher of righteousness.* (II Pet 2:5). Fear of what others may think of us, which Noah resisted for a century, is a common form of cowardice.

However, Post- and Mid-Tribulationists, who do take these matters seriously, may be wasting their time trying to identify the Antichrist already. Paul makes it clear that he will not be revealed until there is a rebuilt temple in Jerusalem: *"Let no man deceive you by any means: for that day shall not come, except there come a falling away first, and that man of sin be revealed, the son of perdition; who opposeth and exalteth himself above all that is called God, or that is worshipped; so that he as God sitteth in the temple of God, shewing himself that he is God"* (II Thess 2:3-4). Initially very few will realise who he really is until he comes to power and makes his seven year covenant; even then only true Bible believers are likely to recognise him. In the meantime there may be more and possibly bigger Nine-Elevens before the Rapture; the President of Nigeria could be right in saying that Boko Haram might export their particular brand of terrorism to Europe. We simply do not know. What we do know is that God knows exactly when this age will end and when earth will enter that brief period, of which Jesus said: *"For then shall be great tribulation, such as was not since the beginning of the world to this time, no, nor ever shall be. And except those days should be shortened, there should no flesh be saved: but for the elect's sake those days shall be shortened"* (Matt 24:21-22).

At the beginning of this book we noted that we would see much about Islamic society and Islamic nations; but that it was not for us to generalise about individuals, each one of whom, like the rest of us, is personally accountable to God. Each should be thought of as a soul who can be won for Christ.

We set out to consider Israel, the Church and Islam, past, present and future. The past simply cannot be changed, although, as we have seen, Muhammad in his Koran did his best to 'correct' whatever recorded history in the Bible he did not agree with. The present is with us; perhaps we can do a little to ameliorate the plight of those suffering from the misdeeds of those representing whichever of the three entities is behaving in the least Godlike way in today's world, and our prayers are perfectly appropriate, especially when offered in a *"Thy will be done"* manner. But it is the future which makes unbelievers fearful. As we have already seen, our Lord foretold a time of *"Men's hearts failing them for fear, and for looking after those things which are coming on the earth"* (Lk 21:26). Christians have no excuse for doubting that God's programme for the future, insofar as it has been declared, is not negotiable, though some have been foolish enough to try to improve upon it – a very serious matter. Of course we have not been given all the details, but we are privileged to have been told a great deal. Thus we can legitimately give brief Bible based summaries; in fact we can quote Scripture with the minimum of comment for both Israel and the Church.

8.2. WHY THE DELAY IN JUDGING?

In recent days I have heard impassioned prayers for those, particularly Christians, suffering from the dreadful persecution inflicted by Islamic Jihadist factions. It is very proper that such prayers should be fervent, and addressed to our God who guarantees to listen when believers pray in the Name of His Son. And one should hesitate in criticising the prayers of fellow believers. But it has sometimes struck me that people are praying as if God's revealed plan of the ages can be negotiated – advanced, postponed or even cancelled - and that all may become peace and light in the world without the personal visible return of the Lord Jesus Christ. We should ever bear in mind, when we pray about such matters, our Saviour's command – and it is a command and not an option – *"And when these things begin to come to pass, then look up, and lift up your heads; for your redemption draweth nigh"* (Lk 21:28)..

Only when one considers the brevity of mortal life in the light of eternity can we begin to perceive why God has allowed evil to

The Future and Personal Options

flourish and his covenant people to suffer. But God is no man's debtor. Habukkuk cries: *"Jehovah, how long shall I cry and thou wilt not hear? I cry out unto thee, Violence! and thou dost not save. Why dost thou cause me to see iniquity, and lookest thou upon grievance? For spoiling and violence are before me; and there is strife, and contention riseth up"* (Hab 1:2-3 Dby). The Psalmist could cry in his misery: *"How long, LORD? wilt thou hide thyself for ever? shall thy wrath burn like fire? Remember how short my time is: wherefore hast thou made all men in vain?"* (Ps 89:46-47); sometimes such cries concerned the supplicant as an individual, sometimes his nation and sometimes evil in general. Sometimes God's answers come quickly; sometimes we are simply required to trust. *"Weeping may endure for a night, but joy cometh in the morning"* (Ps 30:5). So often in the Bible God has allowed his people to express their frustration with His delay in judging and has graciously recorded their words for posterity; but we forget that a frustrating delay for one may be a merciful one for another. Even the souls of Tribulation martyrs awaiting resurrection have their future pleas recorded by John: *"I saw under the altar the souls of them that were slain for the word of God, and for the testimony which they held: And they cried with a loud voice, saying, How long, O Lord, holy and true, dost thou not judge and avenge our blood on them that dwell on the earth?"* (Rev 6:9-10).

Abraham was told by God: *"And thou shalt go to thy fathers in peace; thou shalt be buried in a good old age. But in the fourth generation they shall come hither again:* **for the iniquity of the Amorites is not yet full"** (Gen 15:15-16). Scripture contains many similar examples. We are assured that God always waits for the most appropriate time. He may listen to our pleas and act upon them as He sees fit, but not to our advice! We don't know how many are yet to be saved before His next great intervention at the Rapture; but He does, and exercises the restraint which we could not.

Lewis Sperry Chafer, commenting on II Thess 2:3-10, writes:

> "Paul, standing at the threshold of the new age, could say, **'the mystery of iniquity doth already work'**..... Iniquity had a definite beginning; it runs a well defined course; it comes to a predicted end..... Much sorrow and sin might have been averted had sin been wholly crushed at the beginning; but again we must believe that much more has been gained by the long delayed termination of evil."

He goes on to list various lovely features of this gain. But in the meanwhile we see the mystery of iniquity already at work, intensifying and accelerating its activity even before the Rapture. It is revealed personified in the coming Beast. The present scourge of Jihadism, is surely one of its manifestations, but it is not the only one.

8.3. GOD'S TIMING IS PERFECT

Old Testament saints right up to Simeon and Anna longed for the promised Saviour-Messiah; *"But when the fullness of the time was come, God sent forth his Son, made of a woman, made under the law"* (Gal 4:4). Satan did all he could to thwart God's purposes then, through Herod and the wise men, the slaughter of the innocents, the wilderness temptations, the mob's attempt to throw Jesus over the cliff (Lk 4:29-30), the storm which had literally to be rebuked and so forth.

Now God is winding up this age; the signs of the times confirm this. Satan is mustering his forces, knowing that his time is short for his final assault, for he pays more attention to prophecy than the average Christian. Satan has two groups of targets beloved by God. His beady eye is on Israel with its forthcoming faithful remnant, not all of whom are yet aware of their coming role on earth following the Rapture; Satan's eye is also on the Church, which he knows will vanish from his grasp at the Rapture. But God's purposes move on at His chosen pace, not Satan's. We are still some time away from the point when the controlling triumvirate of the demonic host will compel the armies of the world, like so many suicidal lemmings, to muster for the fatal battle of Armageddon: *"And I saw three unclean spirits like frogs*

The Future and Personal Options

come out of the mouth of the dragon, and out of the mouth of the beast, and out of the mouth of the false prophet. For they are the spirits of devils, working miracles, which go forth unto the kings of the earth and of the whole world, to gather them to the battle of that great day of God Almighty" (Rev 16:13-14). Yet such a scenario has over the last decade or so become ever more realistic with the unprecedented, insane desire of Jihadists to engage in suicidal missions which are designed to cause the maximum destruction, utterly regardless of personal consequences to others.

A rather tasteless joke was circulating recently regarding two mothers of jihadist suicide bombers, where one remarked to the other, "Children, children! How quickly they blow up nowadays"! But it was a fair reflection on common attitudes within Islamic society. And while there is genuine grief on the part of some parents, whose sons or daughters have flown off to join Islamic State or whatever organisation happens to present the best prospects of striking a blow for Allah before being propelled into eternity, there is often a sense of family pride in this needless sacrifice. The murderers see their actions as providing a short cut for themselves to Heaven and for their victims to Hell. What an incredible delusion! As for these victims, if they are truly Christian believers, **their** martyrdom will receive Divine recognition and reward; the *"beheaded for the witness of Jesus, and for the word of God"* are especially singled out as participants in the blessed First Resurrection (Rev 20:4,6). Their demonically duped murderers will have to await the dread Second Death for their eternal fate. *"Write, Blessed are the dead which die in the Lord from henceforth: Yea, saith the Spirit, that they may rest from their labours; and **their works do follow them"*** (Rev 14:13). The suicide bomber's works supposedly buy him or her a place in Paradise; the believer's works cannot purchase what Jesus has already done with His own blood; but their works, when tested, will gain joyful recognition from their Saviour's hand.

8.4. YOUR PERSONAL FUTURE?

If you and I already trust in the Lord Jesus Christ as our Saviour, our future beyond the Rapture is the Church's future, although there is still scope for each one of us before the Rapture to lay up for ourselves further *treasures in Heaven*. As we approach our deathbeds, we do not have to hope that we have 'done enough' or are 'good enough'. None of us is good enough, but He who died in our place was sinless; furthermore, He did it all – paid the price of our sin. And God the Father is satisfied with His Son, and if we trust in Him we have that blessed assurance of sins forgiven and a home in Heaven. The one thing which God will not tolerate is our preferring to make our own imperfect way to Heaven, rather than accepting His perfect way.

Jesus Christ made two statements long ago which still stand: *"Verily, verily, I say unto you, He that heareth my word, and believeth on him that sent me, hath everlasting life, and shall not come into condemnation; but is passed from death unto life"* (Jn 5:24) and *"All that the Father giveth me shall come to me; and him that cometh to me I will in no wise cast out"* (Jn 6:37). Those were the verses that led me as a teenager to faith in Christ. Whether your background is Protestant or Catholic, Shia or Sunni, atheist or agnostic, average sort of person or especially wicked, if you come to Jesus Christ in simple faith, acknowledging your need of Him as Saviour, He will not turn you away, and, when the Rapture occurs, you will be taken to glory. God knows in advance what your response will be, but He still requires you to make the momentous decision for yourself. The very first person to be saved when Jesus was crucified was a criminal, who had had no opportunity to do anything worthwhile after his simple repentance and request to Jesus; three hours later He was dead, but His soul was in Paradise and his body still awaits the glorious First Resurrection (Lk 23:39-43).

The love of Christ should constrain us to preach our Lord's Return. Like other writers on prophecy, I humbly hope that my book may help to point the way of salvation in the new situation

The Future and Personal Options

facing the world. I know that after the Lord Jesus Christ has taken His Church home, copies of this book will be left behind; the title might attract the attention of individuals troubled by the prospect of the unknown.

Supposing you do not turn to Jesus Christ in faith; what then? When the Church is suddenly called home, particularly within what we call Christendom, there will be incredible disruption, as families, communities, organisations and even some churches lose key members. Panic is bound to ensue. In such circumstances the cry will be for direction and leadership. In times of national crisis national leaders are needed and invariably somebody comes to the forefront. But this will be a truly global crisis and a global leader or superman of unprecedented stature will be sought, and will be provided by Satan who will have been grooming him. We have seen that, whatever people on earth think of him, in God's estimation he will simply be a Beast. In modern politics those elected are often proved to have been 'economical with the truth' during their campaigning. But this man will be the representative of the father of lies (Jn 8:44), and he has to be incredibly convincing. Firstly he will have to produce a plausible explanation, other than the truth, for the disappearance of believers, and he is going to succeed with those who have previously heard the Gospel and have deliberately gambled with their souls, because he is described as: *"Even him, whose coming is after the working of Satan with all power and signs and lying wonders, And with all deceivableness of unrighteousness in them that perish; because they received not the love of the truth, that they might be saved"* (II Thess 2:9-10).

As we have already seen in Rev 7:9-14, and repeat here: *"Lo, a great multitude, which no man could number, of all nations, and kindreds, and people, and tongues, stood before the throne, and before the Lamb, clothed with white robes, and palms in their hands..... These are they which came out of great tribulation, and have washed their robes, and made them white in the blood of the Lamb"* (Rev 7:14). Included in this multitude there are likely to be former Muslims, Sikhs, Hindus, Buddhists, atheists and even Christians who have never heard the Gospel. But Scripture gives the strongest hints that not included will be those who have knowingly and deliberately put off being saved in the mistaken confidence that, like the Roman governor of old, they could enjoy sin and change their mind when necessary: *"Now as he (Paul) reasoned about righteousness, self-control, and the judgment to come, Felix was afraid and answered, 'Go away for now; when I have a convenient time I will call for you'"* (Acts 24:25 NKJV). As far as Scripture records, he never did.

8.5. WITNESSING TO MUSLIMS

Satan loves to find Christians 'building bridges' with the world', unless these are meticulously guarded. If such measures are considered essential in military tactics, how much more they are with the most cunning enemy of all! How naïve Christians can be! The wisdom of the world would recommend finding common ground with Islam – building bridges. But this simply gives grounds for assuming that our two religions are at different levels on the same continuum - one rather better or worse than the other. A few churches have even held joint prayer meetings with Muslims – praying to different gods! William Miller, forty-three years a missionary in Iran, is right in saying that we should stress not the similarities, but the contrasts, the differences. We have considered many in these pages; let us recall a few.

- Christianity worships God who gave His beloved Son. Islam worships Allah, who has no son to give.
- Christianity worships a God who revealed Himself in His Son. Islam worships a god who is unknowable and unpredictable.
- Christianity is the religion of Abel – the acceptance of the need of the Lamb to die in our place. Islam is a variation of the religion of Cain; it relies on deeds to appease Allah.
- Christians worship the God who loves lost sinners. Muslims believe in Allah, who loves only those who have first submitted to him.

- Christians derive no special merit from visiting the Jerusalem tomb where angels declared, *"He is not here, He is risen"*. Muslims seek merit in making pilgrimages to what is not an empty tomb, but rather an occupied one of somebody who died more than thirteen hundred years ago.
- Christianity forbids glorying, *"save in the cross of our Lord Jesus Christ"*. A good Muslim may feel justly proud of his devotion, even though it cannot save him.

Sadly much of what calls itself Christianity today fails to live up to these standards.

8.6. WITNESSING TO ALL THREE

Time is running out. We should be feeling the same sense of urgency and conviction as good old Noah; I quote this verse again because there is such an important example for us to learn from: *"By faith Noah, being warned of God of things not seen as yet, moved with fear, prepared an ark to the saving of his house; by the which he condemned the world, and became heir of the righteousness which is by faith"* (Heb 11:7). As Peter reminds us, we should *"be ready always to give an answer to every man that asketh you a reason of the hope that is in you with meekness and fear"* (or reverence): (I Pet 3:15). And remember the lesson Elisha impressed upon his servant – that *"those that are with us are more than those that are with them"* (I Kings 6:16).

Judaism is God-ordained, but was so distorted by men that the majority of its vocal members, such as the Pharisees, crucified the Messiah whom they proclaimed to be waiting for. **When the time came, they chose a terrorist**: *"And they all cried out at once, saying, 'Away with this Man, and release to us Barabbas' -- who had been thrown into prison for a certain rebellion made in the city, and for murder….. And he (Pilate) released to them the one they requested, who for rebellion and murder had been thrown into prison; but he delivered Jesus to their will"* (Lk 23:17-19,25 NKJV). The consequence were inevitable: *"Days will come upon you when your enemies will build an embankment around* *you, surround you and close you in on every side, and level you, and your children within you, to the ground; and they will not leave in you one stone upon another, because you did not know the time of your visitation"* (Lk 19:43-44 NKJV). Many to whom these words were addressed lived to see them fulfilled.

Yet the longing expressed by Paul is as appropriate today as it was then: *"I have great heaviness and continual sorrow in my heart. For I could wish that myself were accursed from Christ for my brethren, my kinsmen according to the flesh"* (Rom 9:2-3); *"Brethren, my heart's desire and prayer to God for Israel is, that they might be saved. For I bear them record that they have a zeal of God, but not according to knowledge"* (Rom 10:1-2). Zeal alone in Jews is no more effective in saving souls than it is in Gentiles: *"I say then, 'Hath God cast away his people? God forbid. For I also am an Israelite, of the seed of Abraham, of the tribe of Benjamin. God hath not cast away his people which he foreknew.'"* (Rom 11:1-2). We Gentiles, whether our background is Christian or Islamic, are the beneficiaries of Jewish rejection nearly two thousand years ago: *"Now if the fall of them be the riches of the world, and the diminishing of them the riches of the Gentiles; how much more their fulness?.....For if the casting away of them be the reconciling of the world, what shall the receiving of them be, but life from the dead?"* (Rom 11:12,15). However we who have turned in faith to the Jews' rejected Messiah have no right to glory in what these others have in the interim period suffered; God has placed a strict time limit on Jewish blindness, a time limit which will run out before Christ's Return in power: *"For I would not, brethren, that ye should be ignorant of this mystery, lest ye should be wise in your own conceits; that blindness in part is happened to Israel,* **until the fullness of the Gentiles be come in**. *And so all Israel shall be saved: as it is written, There shall come out of Zion the Deliverer, and shall turn away ungodliness from Jacob"* (Rom 11:25-26). Those who currently witness to Jews have a share in a blessed work. And the Deliverer, when He comes, will prove to be the very One they rejected (Zech 12:10).

The Future and Personal Options

Christianity recognises and accepts the Messiah whom Israel rejected; Messiah is the Hebrew equivalent of Christ: *"He is despised and rejected of men; a man of sorrows, and acquainted with grief: and we hid as it were our faces from him; he was despised, and we esteemed him not"* (Isa 53:3). But there are still millions upon millions of Bible-believing Christians. Christianity is effective for salvation and eternal life only when in faith we accept that: *"He was wounded for our transgressions, he was bruised for our iniquities: the chastisement of our peace was upon him; and with his stripes we are healed"* (Isa 53:5). Whoever we are, wherever we come from, when we accept that His vicarious death was in our place, then *"He shall see of the travail of his soul, and shall be satisfied: by his knowledge shall my righteous servant justify many; for he shall bear their iniquities"* (Isa 53:11).

Spineless, lukewarm, compromising Christianity makes no impact upon society which has turned its back on its Creator. It will also make no impact upon Muslims. Our Lord's reaction to such churches is: *"I know thy works, that thou art neither cold nor hot: I would thou wert cold or hot. So then because thou art lukewarm, and neither cold nor hot, I will spue thee out of my mouth"* (Rev 3:15-16). No church is immune; the Lord was addressing a church with a high opinion of itself; conservative churches are at least as vulnerable as liberal ones in this respect.

Apostasy, apathy and compromise in countries where it is still comparatively safe to be a Christian impact upon fellow believers in those countries where it is far from safe. We should stop and think about this. Features which our Lord found nauseating in Laodicea may also be repugnant to Muslims, who are thus more likely to feel justified in taking militant counter-measures against such weakness. Anglican Archbishop Eliud Wabukala of Kenya, where Christians face murderous Islamic attacks, especially from Somaliland, reflected widespread disillusionment with the increasingly liberal and permissive 'mother church', led by the Archbishop of Canterbury, and at Easter 2015 voiced the widespread view of African and other evangelical 'Third World' members of the Anglican community, calling for the "restoration of Biblical truth in the face of attacks from Islamic radicalism and an increasingly intolerant secular culture". I am not an Anglican, and recognise that other denominations suffer from the same shortcomings; but I wholeheartedly endorse his call. No denomination's accumulated traditions, hierarchies and bureaucracies should be regarded as sacrosanct. God Himself sanctions and even orders exits on the grounds of conscience: *"And I heard another voice from heaven, saying, Come out of her, my people, that ye be not partakers of her sins, and that ye receive not of her plagues"* (Rev 18:4).

My hope is that, where such returns to Biblical truths do occur, those involved do not fail, like their Reforming forefathers, to eradicate the great Augustinian lie, namely, that all Scripture should be taken as literally as possible, apart from unfulfilled predictive prophecy, which should be taken figuratively or allegorically. Four or five centuries ago the issue was less important. Today its importance is impossible to exaggerate.

Islam at best is a man-made religion. That does not mean that it does not have devout and sincere members who try to lead good lives. The Five Pillars of Islam have certain commendable facets. But, being the religion of the sword, it can encourage fanaticism with the capacity to be fanned into a flame, legitimising in the minds of its devotees bloodshed in its pursuit of expansion. Like the Jews referred to above who chose Barabbas, Islam chose the terrorist and murderer and will bear the inevitable consequences. In the previous section we looked at some of Islam's contrasts with true Christianity, so need add no more.

*****

Although we know that multitudes will never be saved, it is our duty to see every unbeliever as well as believer as a sinner for whom Christ died. Jesus Christ says: *"I say unto you, there is*

The Future and Personal Options

joy in the presence of the angels of God over one sinner that repenteth" (Lk 15:10). As Christians, we can quote that to anyone of any religion when we point to the One who spoke those words. As ambassadors for Christ, we can present the most wonderful means of eternal salvation to the Muslim, the Orthodox Jew, and the nominal Christian, all of whom we must love for Christ's sake. *"Now then we are ambassadors for Christ, as though God did beseech you by us: we pray you in Christ's stead, be ye reconciled to God. For he hath made him to be sin for us, who knew no sin; that we might be made the righteousness of God in him"* (II Cor 5:20-21). What a Gospel, and what a privilege to proclaim it!

Bibliography

The most widely used reference books are shown in **bold** print.

Avi-Dean, Dvorah, *The Jerusalem Ruler* (Sargel Yerushalaim Ltd, Jerusalem, 1999)

Aziz, Sheik Abdul, *From Mohammedanism to Christ* (Central Bible Truth Depot, London c1950)

Barnabusaid (March/April 2015)

Baron, David, *The Ancient Scriptures and the Modern Jew* (Hodder & Stoughton Ltd, London, 1909)

FFM, *A Pocket Guide to Islam*, (Wakefield, W Yorks, 1992)

Baxter, J Sidlow. *The Master Theme of the Bible* (Tyndale House, Wheaton, Illinois, 1973).

Chafer, LS, *The Kingdom in History and Prophecy* (The Bible Institute Colportage Assn, Chicago, 1930)

Darby, JN, *Collected Works – Prophetic Vol II* (G Morrish, London, 1842)

Darby, JN, *Practical Reflections on the Psalms* (Stow Hill Bible and Tract Depot, London, nd)

Davis, Malcolm C, *Anticipating the End Times – Daniel* (John Ritchie Ltd, Kilmarnock, 2010)

Davis, Malcolm C, *Coming Back From Exile* (Precious Seed Publications, Radstock, 2015)

De Silva, J W, *Calvinism; Bitter for Sweet* (John Ritchie Ltd), Kilmarnock, 2014

Ellicott, Charles J, *Bible Commentary for English Readers*, vol I, Cassell Company, London, nd)

Greed, John A, *Prophecies in Parallel* (St Trillo Publications, Portishead, 2007)

Guinness, H Grattan, *The Approaching End of the Age, 13th edn* (Hodder & Stoughton, London, 1897)

Hender, Don, *The Nation of Israel* (Pearl Publishing Press, 2001)

Hislop, Alexander, *The Two Babylons* (B McCall Barbour, Edinburgh, 1998 reprint of 1916)

Hole, FB, *The Gospel of John* (Central Bible Truth Depot, London, nd)

Hunt, Dave, *A Cup of Trembling* (Harvest House Publishers, Eugene, Oregon, 1995)

Kidner, Derek, *Genesis* (Tyndale Press, London, 1967)

Miller, William M, *A Christian's Response to Islam* (STL Books, Bromley, Kent, 1981)

Nuqaiyyah, Waris Maqsood, *Teach Yourself Islam* (Bookpoint Ltd, Abingdon, Oxon, 1994)

Prime, Derek, *Questions on the Christian Faith Answered from the Bible* (Hodder and Stoughton, London, 1967).

Qur'an, translated by Saheen International, Jeddah, 1997

Randles, Bill, *A Sword on the Land*, (St Matthew Publishing Ltd, Huntingdon, 2013)

Rice, John R, *Christ in the Old Testament* (Sword of the Lord Publishers, Murfreesboro, Tenn, 1969)

Riddle, JM, *Ritchie Old Testament Commentaries* – Isaiah (John Ritchie Ltd, Kilmarnock, 2005)

Sookhdeo, Patrick, *A Christian's Pocket Guide to Islam* (Christian Focus Publications, Fern, Ross-shire, 2001)

Sookhdeo, Patrick, *A People Betrayed* (Christian Focus Publications, Fearn, Ross-shire, 2002)

The Times History of the World (Times Books, Harpers Collins Publishers, London, 1999)

Stice, Ralph, *Arab Spring and Christian Winter* (Kindle download, 2014)

Tatford, FA and McNicol, A, *Middle East Cauldron* (Prophetic Witness, Eastbourne, 1971)

Walvoord, John F, *Major Bible Prophecies* (Zondervan Publishing, Grand Rapids, 1991)

Walvoord, John F, *Prophecy Knowledge Handbook* (Victor Books, Wheaton, Illinois, 1990)

Wood, A Skevington, *Signs of the Times* (Oliphants, London, 1970)

Unger, Merril F, *Unger's Bible Dictionary* (Moody Press, Chicago, 1966).

Ye'or, Bat, *The Decline of Eastern Christianity Under Islam* (Fairleigh Dickenson University Press, London), 1996

Young, Paul, *Cunningly Devised Fables* (John Ritchie Ltd, Kilmarnock, 2002)

Other books by Donald Cameron:
Apocalypse Facts and Fantasies (Twoedged Sword Publications, Waterlooville, 2006)

The remainder are published by John Ritchie Ltd, Kilmarnock:
The Day of Vengeance of Our God, 2007
Christian Credibility in a Global Crisis, 2009
The Minor Prophets and The End Times, 2010
End Time Prophecy in the Gospels, 2011
God's Timetable for a Troubled World, 2012
Rapture Sooner Not Later, 2013
The Millennium – Restoration After Retribution, 2014